T0261312

Organizational Design for Knowledge Management

FOCUS SERIES

Series Editor Jean-Charles Pomerol

Organizational Design for Knowledge Management

Mona Ben Chouikha

WILEY

First published 2016 in Great Britain and the United States by ISTE Ltd and John Wiley & Sons, Inc.

ISTE Ltd
27-37 St George's Road
London SW19 4EU
UK

www.iste.co.uk

John Wiley & Sons, Inc.
111 River Street
Hoboken, NJ 07030
USA

www.wiley.com

Library of Congress Control Number: 2015959667

British Library Cataloguing-in-Publication Data
A CIP record for this book is available from the British Library
ISSN 2051-2481 (Print)
ISSN 2051-249X (Online)
ISBN 978-1-84821-922-9

Contents

Introduction

Information and communication technology (ICT) has brought about an increase in the proportion of present-day financial exchanges accounted for by services[1]. We are witnessing a transformation of modern economies, characterized by a very significant role of information and knowledge in the creation of wealth[2]. Knowledge, in the broadest sense, including know-how, constitutes an intangible asset which has a genuine bearing on businesses' survival. Made up of information and know-how, and connected to a context, knowledge gives rise to interpretation and reflection [DAV 98a]. Knowledge may equally be held by individuals [ALA 01] and by organizations [GRA 96b], for which it is an essential resource. Resource theory views knowledge as a strategic tool, which can lend companies a long-lasting competitive edge [PEN 59, BAR 91, TEE 97]. In order to draw benefit from this intangible resource, organizations look for means, methods, procedures, approaches and technical solutions to effectively manage knowledge [CON 96]. In the context of collaboration and interdependence of resources, organizations also make use of strategic alliances (joint ventures), mergers or other legal forms of association which have an impact on knowledge management [YOO 07, BEN 09a].

---

1 From the 1990s onward, the pace of international exchanges of services intensified. Thus, in the decade from 1990 to 2000, the average annual growth rate of such exchanges reached 6% [WTO 01], which is equal to that of goods exchanges. In 2007, services represented around 19% of world trade [WTO 08].

2 The proportion of activities linked to the immaterial (research, education, software industry, etc.) is tending to increase in the world economy [OCD 96]. Such is the case, for instance, in the United States, where the portion of expenses devoted to R&D activities has more than tripled between 1950 and 2000. In addition, between 1990 and 2000, the intensive activities in technology such as electronics, IT, telecommunications and biotechnologies experienced faster growth than the average in other sectors of the world economy [OCD 00].

The process of knowledge management has been described as comprising multiple interlinked activities: gathering, storage, sharing, use and creation of new knowledge [DAV 98a, ZAC 99, CAR 04, BEN 09b]. However, this process is by no means without pitfalls and difficulties. To begin with, professionals dedicate a significant portion of their time and effort to gathering the information necessary to carry out their tasks. Moreover, inter- and intra-organizational mobility and the retirement of the "baby boom" generation entail the loss of skills and knowledge that are often vital for the organizations. In addition to these problems of knowledge-collection and preservation, there is that of knowledge transfer – a problem which is twofold. The first aspect pertains to the difficulty in transferring and distributing tacit knowledge. The second is linked to the tensions between the necessary tacit knowledge management and the behavior of the people who hold that knowledge. Also, these knowledge-management activities do not necessarily automatically lead to an improvement of the organization's performances. The knowledge needs to be assimilated or adapted and applied in new scenarios [CAR 03]. However, it is recognized that there is a difference between what a person knows and what she or he can express and transfer to others. In this regard, Polanyi [POL 67] noted that "we can know more than we can tell". Numerous possible solutions have been put forward to circumvent these difficulties. First of all, organizations tried to encode pieces of knowledge and store them in databases. There are two issues with this solution. To begin with, it is not possible to codify all knowledge – particularly when it comes to tacit knowledge – and second, access to the encoded information is not always easy, which can lead to considerable wastes of time. Next, solutions for knowledge management and collaborative working were proposed, with a view to remedying the shortcomings related to database use. These are knowledge-management systems (KMSs). These tools do seem to have been successful in improving knowledge management, according to Alavi and Leidner [ALA 01]. Nonetheless, there have also been numerous problems with their use, linked to organizational and individual characteristics [MAI 07, BEN 14, BEN 15a]. Thus, a large number of knowledge-management initiatives have failed to achieve their objectives because of the employees' dislike for systematic sharing of knowledge [KAN 05]. Indeed, the time required to enter the data in order to contribute to knowledge bases is a major constraint with this approach [DAV 98a, ALA 01]. It has also been noted that employees were reticent to share their knowledge through such tools, for fear of being dispossessed of their skills and of therefore losing their employability [REN 08]. Consequently, KMSs are often underused [KAN 05].

The main obstacles to the development of knowledge management have been cataloged in the existing literature: a lack of commitment on the part of company directors, a low degree of motivation from the actors within the organization who either hold the knowledge or are potential users of it (largely due to the lack of an incentive system) and a cultural transformation – the difficulty in switching from a culture of compartmentalization and vertical circulation of information to a culture of sharing and trust. Furthermore, while ICT offers quicker access to more extensive and richer sources of knowledge, the fact remains that the holder and the user of a piece of knowledge must be involved personally in its sharing. Indeed, the knowledge holder, as the "teacher", must be convinced of the advantage to exchanging and sharing his or her knowledge and skills [ROB 00] and the knowledge user, as the "knower", must be convinced of the usefulness of assimilating and appropriating the knowledge held by others. The development of knowledge management cannot be reduced to an investment in technologies; it requires close collaborations between the general management, the human resource managers, the business department heads and IT managers, inspired by the desire to transform the organization's practices [REI 04]. This transformation leads to a new professional culture. Although their technological capabilities are formidable, KMSs do not achieve their objectives, because insufficient attention is paid to the social and organizational aspects. Because knowledge (and especially tacit knowledge) lies in individuals' memories and brains [ALA 01], movement of that knowledge is contingent upon those people's motivation and behavior with a view to sharing it. This being the case, personal characteristics need to be taken into account in KMS projects.

The aim of this book is to gain an understanding of, and explain, the conditions which can favor and/or inhibit knowledge management in the organization. In order to do so, we shall identify the conditions in which knowledge can be created, formalized, exchanged and validated. These conditions must take account of the organizational structure, the sociocultural context and the technological infrastructure. Previous literature has focused on studying knowledge management from a particular angle of the organization: strategic, structural, cultural or technological.

By systemic integration, we catalog the determining factors in effective knowledge management. To do this, we draw inspiration from the organizational design [GAL 71, GAL 73, GAL 77, GAL 82, GAL 94, GAL 00a, GAL 00b, GAL 02a, GAL 02b].

In addition to a complete review of the literature on knowledge management, in this book, readers will find an answer to the following two questions:

1. What are the organizational conditions which facilitate and/or inhibit the development of knowledge management among the members of a project team?

2. What role is played, in this development, by KMSs?

To answer these two questions, we have adopted a systemic approach and, drawing upon Galbraith's work of modeling [GAL 73, GAL 02b], which demonstrates interaction between five domains of design of the organization (strategy, incentivization systems, people, processes and structure), we have constructed our own model of a knowledge-oriented organization, called "learning organization design".

As the content of this book is based on research projects, the problems and the results obtained have been validated by a cross-cutting case study [YIN 84, YIN 03b] carried out in a multinational (SCCC) which experienced a merger with a competitor (N) in the same domain. We use the acronym "NSN" to denote the group created by the merger of SCCC and N. Our access to the field for experimentation purposes took place in three stages:

– before the merger: SCCC;

– during the merger: SCCC and N;

– after the merger: creation of the company NSN.

Our research is rooted in the reality on the ground, in order to gain a fuller understanding of the context in which the actors are working and the meaning that they attach to their actions.

First of all, we have chosen to adopt two positions for the study: participative observation and non-participative (passive) observation, which offers a good understanding of the field, a rich dialog with the various people involved and privileged access to a certain amount of data, reflecting a multitude of different points of view [GIO 03]. Then, we opted for the method of analyzing the content of transcribed interviews [MIL 91]. To begin with, this involved analyzing the interviews one at a time, and then a second phase was a thematic analysis. The sequential analyses of each interview helped to identify all of the themes touched upon by the interviewees, and the thematic analysis of all the interviews enabled us to draw up a precise thematic dictionary.

One of the contributions of our research is the employment of Galbraith's model [GAL 73, GAL 02b] in a domain which is truly crucial for organizations: knowledge management. We have integrated the definitive factors in a knowledge-management policy, extracted from a literature review, across the five dimensions of organizational design: strategy, incentivization systems, people, processes and structure.

Our analysis of knowledge management in three periods of an organization's existence (before the merger, during the merger and post-merger), with regard to the same project teams working on the same matters (preparation of bids and elaboration of the solution), yielded results which both concur with and diverge from those demonstrated in the existing body of literature. Indeed, certain conditions put forward in the literature are borne out; others were contradicted; some were entirely absent and new conditions emerged from the field. In addition, when we analyzed the results of the three phases, it was noted that certain conditions are ambivalent.

We have been able to analyze this ambivalence through the lens of different aspects of the idea of culture: national, organizational and professional. Each of these different cultures has a specific kind of influence on individuals' behavior in managing their knowledge. This result is another of the contributions of our research, both in the scientific domain and in organizations' practices. Finally, our case study and the empirical analyses of the process of knowledge management in the organization can contribute to a deeper understanding of this phenomenon, because of the detailed elements it provides. In this way, the new model of organizational design – called the "learning organization design model" – constitutes an instrument that helps to better understand the different aspects of knowledge management in modern organizations.

This book is divided into five chapters (aside from the Introduction and Conclusion), which are arranged in two separate parts:

– Part 1 is devoted to a review of the literature on knowledge management and the theoretical framework of our study – it comprises Chapters 1 and 2:

- Chapter 1 defines the main concepts relating to the issue and lays out the theoretical foundations of knowledge management,

- Chapter 2 begins by presenting the fundaments of our theoretical framework, using the system approach and the organizational design model, before going on to describe our conceptual model called the "learning organization design";

– Part 2 is made up of Chapters 3, 4 and 5 and presents a case study which facilitated the emergence of a new organizational design for the domain of knowledge management: the "learning organization design":

- Chapter 3 outlines the methodological choices, the field of research and the methods of data collection and processing,

- Chapter 4 presents the empirical analyses and the results of the validation of our model during the three phases of our study (before the merger, during the merger and post-merger),

- Chapter 5 discusses the results obtained, comparing them to the literature on knowledge management, and sets out the main conclusions of our work.

Finally, the general conclusion presents the contributions, the limitations and the prospects of our theoretical and empirical work for different academic and professional domains.

Part 1

A Systemic Approach to the Organization Based on
Knowledge Management and its Tools

1

Theoretical Anchoring of Knowledge

Resource theory views knowledge as a strategic asset [GRA 91, BAR 91]. Knowledge resources, which are distributed throughout the organization and are difficult to identify and imitate, are likely to offer a long-lasting competitive edge if used properly [KOG 92, NON 95]. Hence, knowledge appears to be a crucial resource for the organization which needs to be maintained and developed.

Information technology (IT) – for example Internet, Intranet, data warehouses, document management, databases and Groupware – offers improved possibilities to better manage knowledge [ROB 00].

In this chapter, we present the general framework of the research and precisely define what it is that we understand by "knowledge".

First, it is imperative to draw the distinction between the various concepts – data, information, know-how, skill and knowledge – because numerous authors present them as being interlinked but differentiated, while others treat them as being the same thing.

Then, given that learning is a means of acquiring and developing knowledge, and that it is inconceivable to study knowledge without making reference to learning, the second section of the chapter is given over to how to make the transition from individual learning to organizational learning.

Then, in the next few sections, we shall examine the main activities making up the process of knowledge management, the tools supporting knowledge management and the human groups that constitute vectors for the development of knowledge.

Finally, the last section of this chapter will deal with the concept of culture, its presence within organizations in a variety of forms and its connection with knowledge management.

1.1. Individual knowledge and skills

The development of individual knowledge takes place in accordance with the following continuum: data → information → knowledge → skill [PES 06].

1.1.1. *Data*

According to the Larousse dictionary, "data is a conventional representation of a piece of information". In this definition, there is no intention or agenda inherent in data[1], which are codified in accordance with a convention, a natural language or a computer language. For example, when a transmitter uses a convention which the receiver does not understand, the message cannot be understood. According to Prax [PRA 00, PRA 07], data are discrete and objective facts resulting from an acquisition: a measurement taken by a natural or manmade instrument. They may be qualitative or quantitative and serve as the basis for reasoning or for other treatment processes.

1.1.2. *Information*

Larousse states that "information is any event, any fact, any judgment brought to the attention of a particular audience, of varying sizes, in the form of images, texts, discourse or sounds". Information is a piece of data emitted by a transmitter, which makes a difference in that it can be interpreted and used by a receiver [BEN 08]. Indeed, for there to be information, the signal must be perceived and understood. The signal can also generate knowledge or help move forward in the solving of a problem [MAR 09]. In summary, "information is a difference which makes a difference" [BAT 08]. It is a means to construct knowledge, which is essentially linked to human action [NON 95].

Figure 1.1 illustrates the relations between the concepts of "data", "information" and "knowledge".

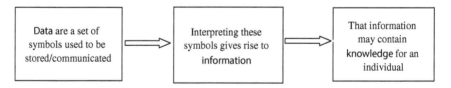

| Data are a set of symbols used to be stored/communicated | Interpreting these symbols gives rise to information | That information may contain knowledge for an individual |

Figure 1.1. *Data – information – knowledge*

---

1 Therefore, data are objective by nature.

1.1.3. *Knowledge*

According to Larousse, "knowledge is what is acquired through study or practice". Various definitions of knowledge have been put forward in the literature published hitherto. The most representative of these are presented in Table 1.1.

Authors	Definitions
Nonaka [NON 94]	Information is a medium necessary for the creation and formalization of knowledge, but information and knowledge are two representations which differ by virtue of where they are located: information is embedded in a message, whereas knowledge exists in human memory. All externalized knowledge becomes information, and all information, when it is interpreted and integrated by a human being, becomes knowledge. All the knowledge held by the individual can be used to help interpret the information received.
Davenport *et al.* [DAV 98b]	Knowledge is information combined with experience, context, interpretation and reflection.
Alavi and Leidner [ALA 01]	On the one hand, knowledge is personalized information, linked to facts, procedures, concepts, interpretations, ideas, observations and judgments. On the other hand, it is the result of a cognitive process.
Carlile [CAR 02a]	Knowledge is a resource which is both critical and difficult to manage. At once, it may be a source of and a barrier to innovation.

Table 1.1. *The various definitions of knowledge*

In the domain of knowledge management, numerous authors agree that knowledge is different from data, information and skill [BOH 94, VAN 97, FAH 98, PRA 00]. Indeed, knowledge is a more complex notion, in that it simultaneously expresses that which is known and the capacity to make use of that information: *savoir-faire* (or "know-how").

Knowledge is a set of schemas – that is dynamic cognitive structures pertaining to concepts, entities or events. These schemas, which are used by the individual to efficiently interpret information, guide the search for, acquisition of and processing of information. They also condition behavior in response to that information. Thus, schemas provide a ready-made system of knowledge. Knowledge is made up of routines which we are able to execute and rules of use indicating when and how to use those routines. More specifically, we can distinguish two types of knowledge: explicit knowledge and tacit knowledge:

– Knowledge, be it explicit or formalized, can be transmitted without loss of integrity through written or oral discourse. For instance, formalized knowledge is the knowledge contained in books or delivered by educational systems. It may just as well be a blueprint or a procedural manual as the content of a database. This codified knowledge can be described and specified in terms of content and intellectual property [COW 97]. It can also be sequential, digital and rationality based, according to Nonaka and Takeuchi [NON 95].

– Tacit knowledge, which is difficult or even impossible to express in a discourse, is not communicated through language. Usually acquired through practice, tacit knowledge often corresponds to contextual situations, to values and implicit standards. This practical knowledge exists at individual level (as an individual's *savoir-faire*) and collective level (e.g. the routines used in the organization and arising from repeated practice). The essential characteristic of tacit knowledge is that it is difficult to pass on, because it is hard to separate the knowledge from the knowledge holder and from its use context. It is acquired through imitation and/or experimentation in a certain context. As specified by Nonaka [NON 94], tacit knowledge includes cognitive elements, schemas, beliefs and mental models defining our view of things and technical elements corresponding *savoir-faire* anchored in specific contexts of action. Polanyi [POL 67] explains that tacit knowledge is personal, closely linked to a given context and, therefore, difficult to transfer.

In Polanyi's view, the tacit and explicit dimensions coexist within any piece of knowledge. The tacit knowledge forms the background which is indispensable to define the structure necessary for the development and interpretation of the explicit knowledge.

This duality (tacit and explicit), introduced by Polanyi [POL 67], has been drawn upon by many authors in discussing the more or less communicable nature of knowledge. For example, Nonaka [NON 91] proposed a dynamic model of the conversion of knowledge from a tacit to an explicit form, and vice versa, known as the "knowledge spiral". Hildreth and Kimble [HIL 02], for their part, note that these two forms of knowledge should not be viewed in opposition to one another, but rather that it is preferable to envisage knowledge with its dual nature. For Nonaka [NON 94], the conversion of tacit knowledge into explicit knowledge and vice versa is necessary for the process of knowledge creation.

1.1.4. *Skill*

There have been many books published on skill which sometimes confuse skill with knowledge.

We can distinguish two categories of works on this topic: those given over to the identification of categories of skills and those devoted to the description of the processes of skill acquisition.

1.1.4.1. *Categories of skills*

Katz [KAT 74] distinguishes three types of skills:

– conceptual skills (analyzing, understanding, acting systematically) – that is knowledge, or "*savoir*";

– technical skills (methods, processes, procedures, specialist techniques) – that is know-how, or "*savoir-faire*";

– human skills in intra- and interpersonal relations – that is existential knowledge, or "*savoir-être*".

In Dejoux's view [DEJ 01], three categories of skills coexist:

– declarative skills;

– procedural skills such as *savoir-faire*;

– diversification skills or judgment skills.

Le Boterf [LEB 01, LEB 02] is at the junction between these two schools of thought, adopting a process-oriented vision and describing the components of skill. In his view, skill is the mobilization or activation of multiple pieces of knowledge, in a given situation and context. This leads him to distinguish six categories of knowledge:

– theoretical knowledge: the ability to understand and to interpret;

– procedural knowledge: knowing how to proceed;

– procedural know-how: knowing what to do and how to operate;

– experience-based know-how: knowing what must be done and how to operate;

– social know-how: knowing how to behave and how to conduct oneself;

– cognitive know-how: knowing how to handle information, how to reason; being able to verbalize what we are doing and to learn.

1.1.4.2. *Skill: a process*

Numerous authors consider skill to be a process. Table 1.2 presents some of the contributions pertaining to this view of skill.

Authors	Definitions
Samurçay and Pastré [SAM 95]	Skill, as the subject's relation with working situations, explains the performance observed by describing the organization of knowledge constructed at work and for the purpose of work.
Cabin [CAB 99]	Skill is latent and is only exercised in a given situation. It is not a state or a possessed piece of knowledge but, instead, is a dynamic process which results from the interaction between several types of *savoirs*: knowledge, *savoir-faire*, *savoir-être* and cognitive functions.
de Terssac [DET 96]	Skill is an intermediary notion which allows us to think about the relations between the work and the knowledge held by individuals.
Prax [PRA 00]	Skill results from the concrete application of knowledge to a particular situation. This requires there to be an evaluative framework and a third-party evaluator.
Le Boterf [LEB 01, LEB 02]	Skill is the mobilization or activation of multiple pieces of knowledge, in a given situation and context.
Beyou [BEY 03]	Skill is the ability to effectively employ knowledge in a given context to produce successful action.

Table 1.2. *Skill viewed as a process*

Thus, skills are:

– finalized: they have a purpose or objective;

– operational: they are effective, which is to say they are employed for specific tasks;

– learnt: they are acquired by various methods and in various forms (training, practice in an activity, etc.).

The concept of knowledge is usually considered to be one of the components of skill. Indeed, knowledge sits between information and skill [PES 06]. In the view of these authors, skills are the final link in a chain, beginning with data, which give rise to information, which produce knowledge, which is integrated into skills (Figure 1.2).

Data → Information → Knowledge → Skill

Figure 1.2. *Links between data, information, knowledge and skill*

Individual skills are the abilities to combine and use the knowledge and *savoir-faire* acquired to deal with situations at work and obtain the expected results. Aptitude, which primarily pertains to people (qualities and capabilities, whether or not they are used), does not necessarily translate into skills. Potential is the set of acquired skills which would enable a person to adapt to new contexts and new situations. The development of individual skills is aimed at the acquisition of *savoir-faire*, knowledge and professional behavior, by an organized, gradual advancement, to enable someone to slowly deal with new professional situations [SAM 95]. In an organization, individual skills can be specified by using a referential framework of the positions involved in the company.

1.2. From individual learning to organizational learning

Individual learning is the basis for the development of collective skills, and the behavior of individuals can influence the effects of learning in the organization [ARG 78]. In addition, individual learning serves as the foundation for organizational learning which, in turn, feeds into further individual learning [ARG 96]. We shall now go on to analyze individual learning and organizational learning in turn.

1.2.1. *Individual learning*

Individual learning is an individual's ability to carry out a task under the influence of the interactions with its environment. Researchers began by focusing on the individual aspects of knowledge and learning, before turning their attention to the organizational dimensions of these phenomena.

The study of individual learning has given rise, first, to a variety of pedagogical approaches and, second, to the conception of different learning styles.

1.2.1.1. *Pedagogical approaches*

The pedagogical approaches arise from work in psychology and pertain to individual learning from the viewpoint of trainers or teachers. We can distinguish three types of pedagogical approaches: the behaviorist approach [SKI 74], the cognitivist approach and the constructivist approach [PIA 79].

1.2.1.1.1. Behaviorism

This approach places emphasis on the external factors in learning: rewards, sociocultural factors, language and the socioeconomic environment [SKI 74]. Impossible to observe, individual mental models may be influenced by the outside world by training and by positive reinforcement (rewards) or negative reinforcement (punishments). The environment is the key element in determining and accounting for human behavior. The individual and his/her own personal representative model are not known to external observers, but they are of crucial importance in knowledge acquisition.

1.2.1.1.2. Cognitivism[2]

This approach reconsiders the above-mentioned environmentalist idea, enriching it with internal factors such as intellectual abilities and personal outlooks. Leading to a modification of the mental structures as experience is gained, learning occurs in different ways, both by sudden understanding (the penny drops) and by the activity of memorization. Given that acquisitions do not necessarily entail the actual emergence of new behaviors, learning takes place when there is acquisition of knowledge giving rise to potential behaviors. Thus, learning lies in the potential for certain behaviors.

1.2.1.1.3. Constructivism

This approach, which was developed in response to behaviorism, emphasizes independent discovery and the importance of trial and error in the act of learning [PIA 79].

The construction of knowledge takes place by action and explanation of the learners' ideas. The individual does not simply receive data as a passive addressee;

---

2 Unlike behaviorism, cognitivism aims to open the "black box" – that is the set of phenomena which take place between the stimulation of the subject by the environment and the organism's observable response. Cognitive psychology was born in the 1950s, around the same time as artificial intelligence (AI). Indeed, once the principle of studying the contents of the black box was accepted, concepts needed to be developed to describe what occurred. The beginnings of computer science saw the development of a conceptual arsenal with which to think about cognition: the notion of information and that of information processing. Extract from Wikipedia.

instead s/he selects and assimilates the data s/he wants to learn about. Following this pedagogical train of thought, learning is not the result of the imprints that sensory stimulations leave in the learner's mind, nor is it the result of conditioning by the environment. Instead, it arises from the learner's activity, whether his/her capacity for action is actual or symbolic, matricial or verbal. This capacity for action of the subject, which arises from personal mental representations, is the result of a dynamic process of finding a balance between the subject and his/her environment. This process may take the form of assimilation or accommodation of the intellectual structures. According to this view, learning is a process of knowledge creation by transformation of one's experience. When faced with a new situation, the subject tries to maintain a balance by integrating that situation into his/her existing mental models (assimilation). When assimilation is not enough to understand the situation, "accommodation" involves the altering of those existing cognitive representations to accommodate the new experience. This process is comparable to the mechanisms of exploitation and exploration identified by March [MAR 91] in organizations.

1.2.1.2. *Learning styles*

The learning process constitutes a cycle which connects thought and action, involving two forms of knowledge acquisition linked to thought and two modes of transformation of the experience linked to action. The four stages in the cycle, in fact, represent the aptitudes required to learn and to solve problems. Thus, four learning styles, based on the pedagogical approaches seen earlier, were defined by Kolb [KOL 84]: assimilation, accommodation, divergence and convergence.

1.2.1.2.1. Assimilation

Assimilation is a learning style characterized by two abilities: reflective observation and abstract conceptualization. The individual tends toward inductive reasoning and tends to have an interest in ideas, abstract concepts, analysis and logic. The strengths of somebody with this learning style are the ability to create theoretical models and learn from his/her mistakes. Weaknesses are a disinterest in realistic solutions and application of theories, the tendency toward reverie and indifference to other people.

1.2.1.2.2. Accommodation

Accommodation is a learning style characterized by active experimentation and concrete experience. In this case, the individual likes doing things, making plans and designing experiments. Strengths associated with such people are their ability to act and react as a function of the facts. Weaknesses are not only impatience and activism but also – because of their perhaps immoderate taste for action – a tendency to do things pointlessly.

1.2.1.2.3. Divergence

Divergence is a learning style characterized by concrete experience and reflective observation. In this case, the individual likes imagining things and approaching concrete situations from a multitude of perspectives. Their strengths are their ability to understand multiple points of view and recognize the possibilities for action in a given context. The main weaknesses of this learning style lie in the difficulty in making decisions, a tendency to become emotionally invested and to ignore or deny conflicts.

1.2.1.2.4. Convergence

Convergence is a learning style which is characterized by abstract conceptualization and active experimentation. In this case, the individual likes applying ideas to concrete situations, finding the right solution, reasoning in a hypothetical-deductive manner, focusing on objects and technique. Strengths for these people are their ability to concentrate their efforts on solving a problem and establishing a plan of action. Their weaknesses lie in their overly hasty choice of a solution, which may lead to the incorrect solution of the problem and a tendency to focus too much on techniques.

1.2.1.3. *Learning loops and conscious states*

In addition to this presentation of the process of individual learning, it is helpful to tie in the concept of levels of learning loops (single-loop and double-loop learning, etc.) and that of conscious states [PRA 97].

The first-level (primary) loop leads to the solution of a problem without the established rules being challenged. The secondary loop comes into play when, in order to solve a problem, it is necessary to critically re-examine the usual structures and rules. A tertiary loop is involved when the very way in which the structures and rules are developed needs to be re-examined. Another aspect of the learning process pertains to the individual's conscious state regarding his/her own knowledge. At the first level, the individual is not aware (conscious) of his/her state of ignorance. In the professional and organizational context, therefore, there is an initial condition which is absolutely crucial in order to begin the learning process: the individuals must not feel threatened by revealing their own state of ignorance. By becoming aware of that state of ignorance, they are then able to engage in the learning process. At the end of the learning process, the individual is conscious of the knowledge that has been acquired. Hence, as the acquired knowledge is activated, s/he will achieve greater dexterity and efficiency and adopt automatic behaviors in carrying out the activity.

1.2.2. *Organizational learning*

The notion of organizational learning, introduced by Simon in the 1950s, has been the subject of numerous publications – often mutually contradictory. According to one view, organizations do not "think" and do not "learn": it is the individuals who learn [MAR 75, SIM 91]. In the view of other researchers, individuals learn individually, but their learning reflects their social context. Thus, organizational learning is more than just the sum of the individual learning [CAR 03]. Teece and Pisano [TEE 94] note that learning is essentially a social process. The internal context influences behavior, cognition, interpersonal processes and group dynamics.

In the eyes of Cyert and March [CYE 63], organizational routines are at the heart of collective learning in organizations; they are a manifestation of the organization's memory which guides the behavior of the individuals and groups within that organization. The process of learning is preserved in the organization's structures, norms and values, which influence individual learning [FIO 85].

In order for there to be organizational learning, there must be at least two individuals, two groups and two organizations. Each person/group transforms the knowledge in his/her own domain of specialty, but at the same time, at the boundaries between them, they are all involved in a process of collective transformation of the knowledge. The upshot of this is that, at the heart of organizational learning, we find relations between actors, differences in knowledge between the actors and the effectiveness of the knowledge situated at the boundaries between the domains of specialization. Therefore, the boundary objects can facilitate organizational learning by reducing rigidity and preventing specialized skills from being restricted to only one person/group [CAR 03].

At organizational level, it is more fitting to speak of "knowledge in the organization" rather than "the organization's knowledge" [MAR 99]. Not everybody in an organization knows the same things. Indeed, there is shared, common knowledge and knowledge specific to one person or to a group of people. Each individual holds specific knowledge which is the fruit of his/her experience, history and intelligence. The use of that knowledge and its evolution take place within the social community that is the organization. This collection of individual knowledge – either private or shared – constitutes the organization's knowledge, which is, therefore, both distributed and diverse. This process of transition from individual knowledge to organizational knowledge is possible by way of dialog, discussion, exchange of experience and observation [NON 95].

Numerous definitions of organizational learning have been put forward in the literature published hitherto. The most representative of these are presented in Table 1.3.

Authors	Definitions
Lave [LAV 93]	It is a creative and collective interpretation of past experiences.
Charreire-Petit [CHA 95]	It is the process whereby old data (knowledge or *savoir*, practices, procedures and representations) are combined with new data and implemented collectively into actions or preparation for future actions. This combination may necessitate the reorganizing, reforming, inclusion or renunciation of practices and/or the principles underlying those practices.
Miller [MIL 96]	It is the acquisition of new knowledge by the actors, who are entirely able and willing to apply that knowledge when making decisions or to use it to influence other members of the organization.
Stata [STA 96]	It is the process by which individuals acquire new knowledge and new understandings and, consequently, modify their behavior and their actions.
Carlile and Rebentisch [CAR 03]	It is a social process involving numerous actors possessing the same knowledge and having conflicting interests. Organizational learning cannot be analyzed as the aggregation of individual learnings.

Table 1.3. *The main definitions of organizational learning*

Analysis of the definitions of organizational learning leads us to summarize them in the following definition, which we shall adopt in our subsequent discussions throughout this book. Organizational learning is a social process which necessarily involves actors who have differing (or conflicting) points of view and interests, whose activities (acquisition–collection, memorization–storage and combination–processing) pertain to a resource (data–information–knowledge–skill). We are deliberately omitting the dimension of the performance expected of effective organizational learning, because this topic is not discussed in this book. On the basis of this brief definition, we feel it is important, in light of our topic here, to touch on the following concepts: organizational memory and the learning organization.

1.2.2.1. *Organizational memory*

Organizational memory[3] is a set of explicit and tacit pieces of knowledge [POL 67], a collective cognitive map of sorts [ARG 78, WEI 79]. The truth of this concept arises from the fact that a large number of organizations have become aware that the knowledge held by their employees is an intangible asset, constituting immaterial capital which lends them a very substantial competitive advantage. The literature on knowledge management varies with regard to this concept of organizational memory in terms of content: information [WAL 91], knowledge [STE 95] and skills [NON 95].

However, analysis of the most significant contributions on this subject leads us to distinguish three types of organizational memory: declarative memory (knowing *what*), procedural memory (knowing *how*) and judgmental memory (knowing *why*). For organizational learning to take place, the organizational memory needs to be extended and updated to support working practices; it needs to be continually reorganized to integrate new information and new concerns [GIR 95].

1.2.2.2. *The learning organization*

An organization learns if, by its processing of information, the range of its potential behaviors is altered. Thereby, it increases the probability that its future actions will lead to an improved performance [HUB 91, HUB 98]. The work of C. Argyris [ARG 95] particularly emphasizes the idea that the effective organizations of the future will be those which are capable of developing their faculty for adaptation, thanks to their ability to learn. The development of learning organizations seems a necessity for modern society. In the author's view, it is crucial to gain control of the defensive routines which stand in the way of change and learning. For Argyris, the organization becomes a learning organization when it helps its members to modify their way of thinking and to learn by constructive reasoning. The employees need to be able to solve not only routing problems linked to "single-loop" learning but also more complex problems when they are faced with working situations they have not encountered before, linked to "double-loop" learning. The process of modification of the routines commits the organization "to learn how to learn" and, thus, to increase its ability to carry out organizational enquiries in order to eliminate the mistakes and inconsistencies which usually occur when the organization/environment system is changed.

Various definitions of the learning organization have been put forward in the literature published hitherto. The main definitions are presented in Table 1.4.

---

3 Also known as collective memory.

Authors	Definitions
Senge [SEN 90, SEN 91]	The learning organization focuses its efforts on the quality of the individuals' thinking, on their shared visions, on their aptitude for reflection, on team-based learning and on the understanding of the complex problems of business life.
Garvin [GAR 93]	The learning organization has a skill to create, acquire and transfer knowledge and to modify its behavior as a function of new knowledge and visions.
Senge *et al.* [SEN 00]	The learning organization is able to develop and use its knowledge to carry out the changes necessary for its long-term survival.

Table 1.4. *Main definitions of the learning organization*

Only the first of these definitions explicitly mentions individuals and human groups. The second definition is centered on the process of organizational learning. The third mentions the aims of the learning organization. Instead of contradicting one another, these three definitions are mutually complementary.

In this book, we shall not touch on the aims of the learning organization but focus only on the conditions of its existence and the processes characteristic of it.

1.3. Knowledge management

The literature, whether academic or professional, defines knowledge management as a process aimed at managing the different phases in the lifecycle of knowledge [CHA 00b, BOU 03, BEC 10, DAL 11]. It involves a set of devices (organizational, incitational, procedural and technological) intended to facilitate the acquisition, conservation and exchange of knowledge (tacit and explicit) between individuals and groups within and outside of the organization [BOU 00].

As Table 1.5 illustrates, the literature has provided numerous definitions for knowledge management.

Authors	Definitions
Hamilton [HAM 98]	A process of creation, transfer and use of knowledge with the aim of improving the organization's yield.
Davenport and Prusak [DAV 98a]	A process composed of the following activities: generation, coding and transfer of knowledge.
Prax [PRA 00]	A process of creation, enrichment, capitalization and validation of knowledge and know-how involving all the actors in the organization, the aim of which is collective performance and the long-term survival of the company.
Ermine [ERM 03]	A process comprising the following activities: capitalization, sharing and creation.
Baile and Lancini [BAI 02a]	An organizational process facilitating the acquisition, structuring, integration and dissemination of actors' knowledge throughout the organization, with the aim of providing a work aid and improving the organization's effectiveness.
Grundstein [GRU 04]	A process designed to amplify the use and creation of knowledge within an organization, with two complementary and strongly interlinked aims: one pertaining to the organization's heritage and one pertaining to sustainable innovation; aims which are underpinned by their economic, human, social and cultural dimensions.

Table 1.5. *The main definitions of knowledge management*

To summarize these definitions, we feel it is useful to return to the concise definition of organizational learning given earlier: "Organizational learning is a social process which necessarily involves actors, possibly in conflict, whose activities (acquisition–collection, memorization–storage and combination–processing) pertain to a resource (data–information–knowledge–skill)".

Like organizational learning, knowledge management is a process. Its social dimension is less prominent, and its activities more precise and presented as necessary to achieve better performance. It arises from this that knowledge management involves deliberate and structured organizational learning. In this book, we consider knowledge management to be a process made up of five interdependent activities, functioning in a loop (acquisition, storage, transfer, application and creation of new knowledge). This iterative nature of the knowledge management process is not new, as Carlile and Rebentisch [CAR 03] and Carlile [CAR 04] mentioned in their work on the knowledge transformation cycle. In their view, the evolving nature of knowledge means that it must be transformed whenever it is used, because the situations encountered are always new, and it is not enough to draw on past experience to overcome knowledge barriers, which constitute obstacles to the sharing of knowledge between individuals and groups of individuals. However, if it proves necessary to employ a common language and lexicon, the common knowledge used often needs to be transformed in order to facilitate the sharing and evaluation of knowledge at the boundaries [CAR 04].

1.3.1. *Knowledge acquisition*

The phase of acquisition or collection of knowledge corresponds to the development of new content or the replacement of existing content in the organization's explicit and tacit knowledge. This collection or acquisition of new knowledge corresponds to a phenomenon of organizational learning which develops on the basis of the knowledge available in the organization (by experimentation, imitation, observation and research). Hence, this learning is rooted in collaborative social interactions, or in individual cognitive processes, given that the knowledge sought may be held by individuals or incorporated in processes and/or artifacts [CAR 03]. The process of knowledge seeking can be described in terms of research [MAR 58, CYE 63] and knowledge acquisition [HUB 91].

Knowledge research involves identifying the knowledge that is likely to satisfy a need or help solve a problem. In order to do this, two iterative tasks need to be completed. The first is to determine the useful sources of knowledge, and the second is to evaluate those sources and determine their relevance for performing the task in question. These two iterative efforts take place in two overlapping spaces: the search space and the solution space. The shape and size of the former is constantly evolving, as newly acquired knowledge opens up new avenues of research and shuts other ones down. The shape and size of the solution space varies as a function of the size of the search space and the requirements to be satisfied. The relation between these two spaces is defined by the process of evaluation of the relevance of the knowledge discovered [CAR 03]. An existing piece of knowledge is useful only when it is sought by individuals, who use it to create value. The search for knowledge, therefore, is motivated by value creation and conditioned by the characteristics of the individuals and groups involved in the action.

1.3.2. *Knowledge storage*

Once acquired, knowledge needs to be preserved. Both at individual and collective levels, it is necessary to preserve it in memory in order to use it afterward. First, storage consists of gathering and preserving, in a use state, the knowledge acquired or created by the organization; second, it involves preventing the loss of knowledge due to forgetting, to turnover or to incorrect identification of the relevant knowledge in the organization. For individuals, knowledge is stored in their memory. At the collective level, knowledge storage refers, by analogy, to the idea of organizational memory. Organizational knowledge is distributed, between different individuals within the organization [WAL 91].

Whether intentional or otherwise, knowledge storage is a process that leads to the accumulation of knowledge. The knowledge accumulated can be contained in files or documents, incorporated in tasks and artifacts or materialized in the experience of individual members of a practice community or a professional group. The nature of the activities and routines of the individuals and groups are crucial factors for the knowledge to be stored. The proliferation of new phenomena provides opportunities to modify or increase the stores of accumulated knowledge. Whether stored intentionally or otherwise, the knowledge is a source of competitive advantage if it can be reused to improve the organization's efficacy or reduce the cost of research, transfer and/or transformation of knowledge. On the other hand, without new phenomena, there are no (or very few) opportunities to acquire new knowledge, because activities can take place on the basis of the knowledge already acquired.

The accumulation of knowledge is linked to the learning curve [ARG 90]. However, in a dynamic environment, the new addition can render obsolete the knowledge stored in the current cycle of activity. Knowledge storage may, therefore, be an obstacle to innovation. Meanwhile, in a stable environment, with little novelty, knowledge storage may be passive and random and may overlook important facts. In addition, knowledge may be stored inadequately, causing it to be forgotten or unavailable, in spite of its potential usefulness and relevance for future applications and decisions [CAR 03].

1.3.3. *Knowledge transfer*

One of the major objectives of knowledge management is to handle the transfer of knowledge between various sources and addressees, at different levels: between individuals, between individuals and groups, between groups of individuals, between groups of individuals and the organization and between organizations [BEN 11, BEN 12]. This process of communication of knowledge can take place through informal channels (spontaneous discussion, informal meeting, etc.), formal channels (training session and formal meetings), personal channels (individual learning from a teacher or in a group) and impersonal channels (use of databases).

Knowledge transfer is a function of the type of knowledge to be transmitted, the nature of the sources and addressees and the context of dissemination, the organizational culture, which may be more or less oriented toward communication and sharing, and incentive systems toward the dissemination of the knowledge. Recognized as more difficult, the dissemination of tacit knowledge requires first an element of explanation by the knowledge holder and second an element of learning, imitation and interiorization by the receiver of the knowledge. Another obstacle to the dissemination of the knowledge is at the source of the transfer process and relates to the identification and localization of knowledge in organizations [HUB 91, HUB 01].

The transfer of knowledge between organizational actors, between groups of organizational actors or between organizational units contributes to the integration of the knowledge [ARG 00, CAR 03]. Knowledge transfer is an iterative process comprising three stages: acquisition, storage and research. The iterative nature of the process arises from the link between knowledge storage and research. Hence, knowledge transfer may have a positive or negative effect at each cycle [CAR 03]. If the new requirement for a solution matches the firm's past activities, then the firm's stored knowledge can be reused. On the other hand, if the new requirement falls outside the field of the firm's past activities, the firm's stored knowledge may become an obstacle and a source of inflexibility. Consequently, the amount of novelty introduced between the moments of storage and of searching for knowledge is a challenge for the integration of knowledge.

1.3.4. *Knowledge application*

The activities of acquisition, storage and dissemination of knowledge do not necessarily yield an improvement in the organization's performances. Only the application of that knowledge into action can deliver some kind of improvement. However, there is often a significant gap between what organizations know and what they do. There may be several reasons that explain why acquired knowledge is not used:

– lack of confidence in the source of the knowledge;

– lack of time to use the new knowledge (it is preferable to use old practices which are tried and tested);

– risk aversion (transposition of knowledge to a different situation to that which led to it entails a risk of error).

In order for the application of knowledge to be effective, knowledge gleaned from different sources needs to be integrated. The diversity of the knowledge needing to be integrated means that this integration is a complex – and, therefore, necessarily iterative – task. According to Carlile and Rebentisch [CAR 03], the complexity of knowledge integration increases with the number of dependencies between the groups or specialized domains in question. When the repetition of the knowledge integration cycle is accompanied by a change in circumstances, the activity of knowledge integration becomes even more complex. Indeed, not only must we integrate the knowledge held by different partners in different domains of specialty, but also we must first determine what the relevant knowledge is to deal with the new needs and by whom that knowledge is held. The integration of knowledge is, therefore, no longer a simple knowledge transfer but an iterative task that includes the establishment of agreements and consensus between interdependent groups. The intensity and number of dependencies between the different knowledge sources, therefore, appears to be a challenge for the integration of knowledge.

In the case where the context of integration of knowledge is stable, the language, methods and artifacts common to the different knowledge sources are defined through repetitive interactions, facilitating fluid communication between the different partners [LAW 67, GAL 73]. In a constantly changing and competitive environment, the high degree of novelty causes strong dependencies and differences between the different knowledge sources. It then becomes necessary to transform this knowledge. However, the dependencies and differences caused by a high degree of novelty lead to new constraints, which constitute obstacles to the transformation of the knowledge. In their activity of knowledge integration, therefore, organizations need to understand what is new and, at the same time, change their existing knowledge to facilitate the creation of new knowledge, necessitating the contribution of multiple domains of specialization [CAR 02a, CAR 03].

1.3.5. *Creation of new knowledge*

The efficiency of implementation of the aforementioned four activities (collection, storage, transfer and application) often engenders a new activity recently studied in the literature: the creation of new knowledge. Knowledge creation allows the organization to survive and deal with the competition by innovation. Creating new knowledge is a significant challenge for organizations [CAR 03, BEN 09a]. The creation of new knowledge disturbs the existing relations between the domains of specialization, which means that the dependency relations between the domains of specialization and the groups of individuals holding the knowledge in those domains need to be renegotiated. This requires time and effort to define a new language, new methods, and new artifacts shared by the different groups contributing to the creation of a product or service.

The acquisition, storage, transfer and iterative use of knowledge and the creation of new knowledge constitute a perpetual cycle of linked activities. Thus, the knowledge management process can be represented diagrammatically by the knowledge management cycle (Figure 1.3).

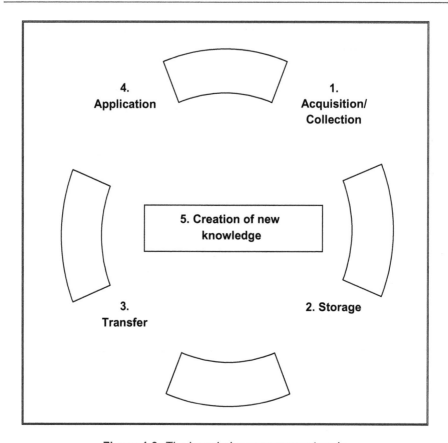

Figure 1.3. *The knowledge management cycle*

In summary, knowledge management refers, first, to the idea of a process in which the number of activities can vary as a function of the organizations and, second, to the operationalization of those processes with resources and tools which fit into a fair balance between the organizational and the technological aspects [DAV 98a]. In the views of these authors, any knowledge-management project must combine a technical infrastructure based on information and communication technology (ICT) and a human infrastructure based on a network of interacting individuals.

We can conclude from these that in order to establish effective knowledge management, it is necessary to:

– identify, compile, save, integrate and create knowledge that is pertinent for the organization;

– facilitate real and virtual exchanges between individuals by integrating the logic of the knowledge transformation cycle [CAR 03, CAR 04];

– implement knowledge management at individual level and at collective and organizational levels.

On the basis of these considerations about the nature of knowledge, which is firmly rooted in the individual as a subject, we can deduce that knowledge management notably involves management of the conditions in which the knowledge can be created, formalized, exchanged and validated.

With the aim of continually improving the process of knowledge management, organizations are increasingly turning to ICT to support the activities involved in this process [ROB 00]. The increasing role of ICT in knowledge management has resulted in the development of knowledge management systems (KMS). Section 1.4 is devoted to the presentation of KMS.

1.4. Knowledge management systems

The different components of KMS are known [BEN 15a]. It is the technological infrastructure, the social structure of the organization and the managerial system governing it. KMS includes one facet corresponding to the exchange of information and/or data between the human operator and the technological infrastructure. A second facet of KMS corresponds to the social interactions which are created via the computer platform by way of exchanges of information, points of view, interpretations, *savoir-faire*, etc.

Thus, there are similarities between KMSs and information systems (IS), such as both include a computer platform and involve human subjects who interact with the system.

1.4.1. *Information systems*

The concept of an IS has been the subject of numerous definitions put forward by researchers and professionals. We can subdivide these definitions into two categories, depending on whether or not they integrate the human factor (the users of the IS).

Apart from fully automated systems which support certain industrial processes, human actors play a critical role in the operation of ISs. In addition, we focus solely on the definitions of an IS which take the human factor into account. Table 1.6 gives a few representative examples of those definitions.

The first [DAV 85] and the second definitions [HIR 95], which do not take account of the organization, are not appropriate for the issue discussed in this book. The same is true of the third definition. Indeed, the third definition [REI 00] does not include the information processing, while the second [HIR 95] includes neither the processing nor the transformation of the information. We shall work on the basis of the fourth definition [MAR 09] but specify that – in this definition – the word "representations" implicitly includes the concept of knowledge and meanings, which is not so with the second definition [HIR 95] which explicitly mentions interpretation and meanings.

Authors	Definitions
Davis *et al.* [DAV 85]	An integrated user–machine system which produces information to assist human beings in the functions of execution, management and decision-making.
Hirschheim *et al.* [HIR 95]	A set of social interactions aimed at creating, exchanging and interpreting meanings.
Reix [REI 00]	An organized set of resources: hardware, software, personal, data, procedures enabling us to acquire, process, store and communicate information within organizations.
Marciniak and Rowe [MAR 09]	A system of social actors who memorize and transform representations by using IT and operating methods.

Table 1.6. *The main definitions of an IS*

1.4.2. *The characteristics of a knowledge management system*

KMS are IS devoted to the management of the knowledge resource. These systems are designed to facilitate the activities of acquisition, storage, transfer, use and creation of knowledge. A KMS is composed of a computer-based infrastructure and a sociotechnical system made up of people (users) interacting via the computer platform.

Table 1.7, which is adapted from Alavi and Leidner [ALA 01], shows that the potential contributions of IT to the processes of knowledge management are extremely varied.

Actual use of a KMS involves two voluntary actions on the user's part [MON 08]: first, consultation of the system to look for useful knowledge and, second, deliberate capitalization upon the new knowledge through the support tool. However, the existence of KMS does not guarantee the success of a knowledge-management strategy implemented by an organization. It is in the use of the KMS and of the influencing factors imposed by the organizational context that the success of knowledge management resides.

Knowledge management process	Knowledge creation	Knowledge storage	Knowledge dissemination	Knowledge application
Tools making up KMS	- Data mining tools - Learning tools - Intelligent agents - Discussion forums - Groupware tools	- Electronic dashboards - Knowledge warehouses - Databases - EDM: electronic data management tools	- Electronic dashboards - Discussion forums - Knowledge warehouses	- Expert systems - Flow management systems - Computer applications
Roles of KMS	- Combination of new knowledge sources - Learning	- Support of individual and organizational memory - Access to inter-group knowledge	- More extensive internal network - More available communication channels - Quicker access to knowledge sources	- Knowledge applicable in multiple situations - Quicker application of new knowledge through workflow automation
Communication Technology Platform Technological – Groupware – Intranet				

Table 1.7. *The functions of KMS depending on the activities of the process of knowledge management [ALA 01]*

Numerous works have been produced on the determining factors of the adoption of KMS [LAN 01, LAN 03, BEN 14], the reuse of knowledge [MAR 01, WAT 06], the factors facilitating contribution behaviors in a KMS [BOU 04a, BOC 05, BEN 10a], the dynamics of insertion of those systems in organizations [ORL 00] and the identification of the structural conditions favoring knowledge management [JOS 02]. The reasons for actors' unwillingness to share via KMS arise mainly from the problems of adhesion to the voluntary capitalization of knowledge [ALA 01], to the formalization of the knowledge and to its reuse [MAR 01, WAT 06]. Indeed, individuals capitalize upon knowledge for themselves but are reticent to capitalize upon it for others' benefit. In order to deal with the problem of sharing, numerous authors have highlighted the necessity of instituting a culture of sharing and an atmosphere of trust in the company [GUR 99, DET 04, GRU 04, KIN 07b, BEC 10, ANA 11, WIE 13, VAN 14]. This problem is linked to individual or subjective factors [MAR 01, LAN 01, LAN 03] based on a give-and-take logic [BOU 00], on opportunistic attitudes [FUL 04] and on organization factors [MAR 01]. In this regard, Hansen *et al.* [HAN 99] distinguish two types of knowledge-management strategies: those which are based on the human (social) network and those which use a KMS. For his part, DeFélix [DEF 02] notes that knowledge management is still a matter of context and actors. This observation demonstrates the need to take better account of the human factor – that is the characteristics of the users, their behaviors, their needs and their requirements. Indeed, IT offers quicker access to more extensive and richer knowledge sources, but the effort of appropriation and assimilation of that knowledge falls to the user of the KMS. The development of knowledge management cannot be reduced to a problem of use of ICT: it requires strict collaboration within the organization, notably involving the board of directors, the heads of human resources, the department heads and the IT department, who must all be motivated by the desire to greatly alter the organizational and cultural practices [REI 04]. In other words, the problems linked to knowledge management and to the use of its tools can only be dealt with by the development of cooperative relations between the actors in the organizations. Indeed, only such cooperation can facilitate the passage of knowledge from individual level to organizational level. By transposing, to the field of knowledge, the analytical results found by Argyris and Schön [ARG 96], showing that "individual learning serves as the foundation for organizational learning which, in turn, feeds into further individual learning", we can say that individual knowledge serves as the foundation for organizational knowledge, which, in turn, feeds into further individual knowledge, which enables the individual to create new knowledge. Nonaka [NON 94] highlighted the complementarity between these two levels of learning and knowledge and stressed the importance of socialization and of exchanges between individuals in order to facilitate the passage from one level to the other. Such socialization and exchanges do exist, regardless of their importance, in any working relationship.

1.5. Communities, teams and knowledge management

The areas of management pertaining to teamwork and knowledge are increasingly close together. The fact that knowledge is a critical resource for the organization to obtain a lasting competitive edge highlights the role of the mechanisms of coordination to integrate the specialized knowledge of the different actors within the organization [GRA 96a]. Nonaka and Takeuchi [NON 95] stress the importance of teamwork in the conversion of tacit individual knowledge into organizational knowledge. The most commonly cited fora for the development of knowledge in organizations are communities and teams [BEN 07, BEN 10a, BEN 15b].

However, there is a wide variety of communities and teams working within an organization, and academic and professional literature on these concepts is rich. In the next part of this chapter, we discuss the most representative of these contributions and illustrate the links between these notions and knowledge.

1.5.1. *Communities*

A community is a group of people who share something: a product, a resource, an obligation, a debt, etc. Although there are many different types of communities, we generally speak of human communities, in the historical or sociological sense. The use of the term "community" generally carries with it the notion of sharing common values. The literature distinguishes several types of communities: professional communities, communities of practice and virtual communities.

1.5.1.1. *Professional communities*

Professional communities formally or informally bring together people of the same profession, whether or not they belong to the same organization. They may constitute a space for collective intelligence, innovation and collective knowledge creation which is not restricted to the jurisdictional boundaries of an organization or a production unity. Often, these communities are organized into professional associations, such as the AFITEP or PMI (for project managers and directors), ASLOG (for logisticians) and CIGREF (for company directors of ISs).

1.5.1.2. *Communities of practice*

Communities of practice are groups of people who share a concern, a set of problems or a passion for a subject, and who extend their knowledge and expertise in that domain by regularly interacting with one another [WEN 02, DAM 05]. In spite of its clarity, this definition covers groups of very variable size, lifespan, homogeneity, location, degree of intentionalization and formalization [WEN 02]. Given so broad a definition, it is difficult to qualify a particular group as a community of practice, and it is sometimes easy to get lost in the jungle of examples described in the literature, ranging from the professional community to the members of a department. Wenger [WEN 98b] distinguishes three aspects which can be used to characterize a community of practice: the mutual commitment of the members, the existence of a common goal and the production of a shared repertoire. *Mutual commitment* involves a relationship between the participants of helping one another, which is necessary for the sharing of knowledge about practice. The *common goal* involves a more or less precise objective. The *shared repertoire* includes physical media such as files or forms and less tangible elements such as gestures, words or protocols.

A group whose cohesion is not based on the combination of these three dimensions would obviously be excluded from the category "community of practice". However, as Chanal [CHA 00a] notes, these dimensions are not sufficient to enable us to clearly distinguish a community of practice. Indeed, a project team is founded on the same mechanisms. Wenger and Snyder [WEN 00] also give us some reference points in the form of a "counter-relief" definition of what a community of practice is *not*. First of all, a community of practice is not a working group or a project team, because in these two structures, the members are appointed by the management, whereas "belonging to a community of practice is self-appointed". In addition, the agenda and the subjects dealt with by communities of practice are defined not by the management but by the members of the community. Next, the lifespan of a community of practice is indeterminate. The identity aspect, according to Wenger [WEN 98b], differentiates a community of practice from a business network. If the network is at the origin of the community, it is simply *"burnt kindling"* [WEN 98a, WEN 98b, GON 01]. Despite the various attempts made by the founders of the concept, it also seems there is a danger of confusing communities of practice with professional communities [VAA 02]. This type of group is distinguished, operationally, both by its size and by the way in which it operates or the diversity of its members. Finally, while communities of practice may be supported by the development of technological tools [VAA 00, WEN 03], they must not be confused with virtual communities, which arise from purely electronic interactions [RHE 93].

Carlile and Østerlund [CAR 05] base their work on those of Lave and Wenger [LAV 91], Brown and Duguid [BRO 91] and Wenger [WEN 98a, WEN 98b], to distinguish the knowledge shared between communities of practice from the knowledge shared within a community of practice and to identify the practices that facilitate knowledge-sharing between communities of practice and those which facilitate knowledge-sharing within a community of practice. In particular, these authors discuss the problem of knowledge-sharing within a community of practice and between several communities of practice by associating it with the use of boundary objects [CAR 02a, CAR 04], and of boundary practices and processes [WEN 98a, WEN 98b], of inter-community fora, translators and knowledge brokers [BRO 98].

1.5.1.3. *Virtual communities*

Virtual communities are sociocultural groups that emerge from the network when a sufficient number of individuals participate in public discussions over a sufficiently long time, being sufficiently motivated for webs of human relations to be woven in cyberspace [RHE 93]. This definition confirms the existence of a virtual space and the idea that virtual communities, which have arisen from the Internet and its increasingly widespread use, constitute entirely separate social facts (e.g. "*chats*" and online discussion forums). Virtual communities distributed across the whole planet are the result of electronic social interactions whose members are freed from the constraints of time and space [JOS 04].

1.5.2. *Teams*

A team brings together a set of people whose tasks are mutually interdependent, who have a common objective which necessitates a certain amount of collaboration between them and sharing the responsibility for their results [COH 97]. That team may be permanent or temporary.

1.5.2.1. *Permanent working teams*

A permanent working team may be a service or a department with the objective of managing operations and ensuring the fulfillment of one part of the organization's mission. The duty of a department, in the organization of a company, is to manage a set of processes, a resource, a function or a "business unit". Depending on the complexity, the reactivity needed and the criticality of the tasks needing to be performed, KMS may be used in permanent teams. Such is the case, for instance, with certain customer-contact centers or "helpdesks" for computer users.

1.5.2.2. *Temporary working teams*

There are various categories of temporary teams, but the most commonplace is the project team.

A project can be defined as a specific, new action, of limited duration, which methodically and progressively lays the foundations for a future reality. A project is a complex system of contributors, resources and actions set up to provide a response to a request made in order to satisfy a need [AFI 92]. The activity of project management includes two subactivities. First, there is the task of project leading, which consists of coordinating the various subprojects and the different stakeholders, reporting to those stakeholders on the overall progress of the project and communicating with them about the milestones reached and the resources being mobilized. Second, there is the task of internal management of the project (project supervision). Generally, there is one project manager and one or more project supervisors in the case of complex projects which are divided into subprojects. On the other hand, with reasonably-sized projects, the project leading and project supervision are done by the same person: the project manager.

The project is run by a project manager, whose hierarchical level and title depend on the importance of the project. Assisted by a team, this leader is responsible for the proper execution of the project in accordance with the wishes of the client (internal or external). For large-scale projects, there are often two interacting authorities: the project leader (PL), representing the client, and the project supervisor (PS), representing the internal or external engineers.

The project management provides the PL and the PS with all the necessary elements to make directional decisions in good time. The purpose of these decisions is to respect the elements of the project brief, in terms of content, quality, time and cost. Thus, project management is mainly to do with making informed projections and predictions and involves a technical, contractual and commercial understanding of the project and a relevant IS. The project team includes a certain number of people of different levels and different professions, with the aim of making a goal (material or immaterial) a reality.

Project teams constitute an interesting area of study when looking at cooperative relations between individuals in the context of knowledge management. First, there is a time limitation on the dynamics of the relations between individuals – all the more so because the turnover rate of contributors may be quite high. This means that knowledge transfer takes place rapidly, whether or not it is supported by tools. Second, the interdependence between the members of a project team is accentuated because of the time constraint. In addition, the actors have different skills. The combination of these last two elements necessitates strong cooperation and intensive communication between the members of a project team. Finally, as the project involves at least a certain amount of innovation, it is often the case that new knowledge is developed even in the course of the action. In addition, Carlile and Rebentisch [CAR 03] and Carlile [CAR 04] note the existence of knowledge barriers – constituting obstacles to the sharing of knowledge – between the different groups making up a project team and belonging to different areas of specialty.

The management of these barriers requires the creation of common knowledge, shared between these different groups. That shared knowledge may result from:

– a simple knowledge transfer when the conditions are stable;

– the creation of common interpretations when something new comes to light;

– the transformation of the different actors' specific knowledge in case of a major novelty.

The power relations between the different actors may have negative consequences on knowledge creation in a project team. These power relations manifest themselves when, at a given time, an actor or group of actors belonging to the project team holding more power than the others imposes their point of view. These powerful actors thus often tend to reuse their past knowledge instead of updating it. Power relations also become apparent over time when the choices made at the earliest stages of the project are imposed during the later stages without taking account of the constraints inherent to those stages.

1.6. Knowledge management and cultures

A survey of 431 European and American organizations shows that culture – be it national, organizational or professional – is the most important determining factor in knowledge management [RUG 98]. Cultural barriers can constitute a major obstacle for effective knowledge management [MCC 04, ANA 11, WIE 13, VAN 14]. Consequently, culture is both important and problematic for knowledge management. The predisposition and willingness of the organizational actors to participate meaningfully in knowledge creation and to share their knowledge with other organizational actors is a crucial factor for the effectiveness of knowledge management, which is heavily influenced by the cultural origins. According to King [KIN 06], culture and knowledge management exert reciprocal influences on one another.

Numerous definitions of culture have been put forward in the existing literature. One of the most general of these is that given by Hofstede [HOF 80], which holds that "culture is a collective mental programming specific to a group of individuals". In spite of their difference, these definitions emphasize the fact that culture consists of a set of values, knowledge, techniques, means of expression and communication shared by a collective or a population. One of the characteristics of the culture of a community is its language, which may be a regional dialect, a national language, or a professional lexicon. Culture comes into play at different levels of a society, company, profession, social class, country, region or religion. That is why we speak of company culture, judicial culture, English culture or Muslim culture. Whatever the community we take as a reference, culture is acquired by education, training and social learning within the community.

Over the past two decades, researchers and professionals have turned their interest to organizational culture and subcultures of the different communities of which an organization is composed. The advantage of studying the impacts of culture relates to the different strategies and tactics deployed by organizations to manage rare resources: pooling of resources, joint ventures, merger/acquisitions and knowledge management [WEI 03].

In addition, we frequently see the concept of culture emerge in the literature on knowledge management, by way of the terms "culture of knowledge sharing" or "knowledge culture" [KIN 07b]. Similarly, there are many references to organizational culture, national culture and organizational climate in the literature on knowledge management [ARD 06, BOC 05, DEL 02, LAN 04, LOP 04, ORD 04, PAR 04].

Three culture profiles have been identified in the literature on organizations: national culture, organizational culture and professional culture.

1.6.1. *National culture*

While culturalist approaches have been the subject of numerous developments, the work of G. Hofstede and P. d'Iribarne is often cited in the literature on international cultural management. A forerunner in the domain of managerial implications of national cultures, Geert Hofstede listed four dimensions which can be used for classification of cultures: hierarchical distance, degree of masculinity, degree of individualism and attitude to uncertainty. On the basis of the principle that the behaviors which characterize a national social system are necessarily replicated within an organization, this author shows that Latin regions such as Latin America and Arab countries are characterized by a long hierarchical distance. On the other hand, English-speaking and Nordic countries such as the Netherlands, the United Kingdom, Sweden and Norway are characterized by a short hierarchical distance, and other countries, such as the USA, Japan and France, have a medium hierarchical distance. The hierarchical distance can be used to understand the relations between the supervisor and his/her subordinates in an organization. It enables us to define certain behaviors to be adopted in the face of the hierarchy or with foreign interlocutors.

The attitude in the face of uncertainty serves as an indicator to help us understand certain behaviors and attitudes toward risk-taking, innovations and foreigners. Countries such as France, for example, which are characterized by low comfort with uncertainty, show significant resistance to change and are, therefore, strongly attached to the drawing up of a long-term plan. In these countries, we also note that the activities linked to risk-prevention, such as the insurance market, are highly developed in comparison to other cultures.

The degree of individualism is highly important in understanding incentive systems. Thus, the Japanese, who are characterized by a collectivist culture, move as a group and are determined that the interests of the group should always prevail over individuals' interests. Therefore, the members of a collectivist culture will be more loyal to their company than those of an individualist culture.

The criticisms leveled at the work of G. Hofstede [HOF 80, HOF 90] essentially relate to the legitimacy of the method of identification of these four dimensions, whether they are equally important from country to country [HAM 97] and the hypothesis that IBM employees can be taken to be representative of the population of a country [CHO 94, HUN 81]. In spite of these criticisms, Hofstede's work exhibits the advantage of providing elements of a panoramic vision of the different cultures.

Trompenaars [TRO 98] also presents a classification of cultures with seven behavioral dimensions. His work can be used as an analytical framework which compliments that of Hofstede. His classification allows a high degree of operationalization of international consultancy firms specializing in inter-cultural issues. In the view of this author, universalist cultures favor rules over relations, unlike particularist cultures. Certain cultures value the statuses given by their institutions: diplomas from a certain school, the age, the genre, etc. It is highly important to pay attention to that aspect when one comes from a culture which values results. Emotions and expressions are also determined by the culture. Certain cultures value public expression of feelings, while others condemn it; as such, expression is thought to be indicative of a lack of self-control. If one comes from a rather emotive culture, such as Italian culture, it is important to avoid looking ridiculous in the eyes of an interlocutor from a culture that disapproves of displays of emotion.

While according to G. Hofstede culture works like mental software which shapes the psychological structures from which the behaviors arise, in P. d'Iribarne's view, it arises from the sedimentation, over a long period of time, of national traditions which govern the ways of acting: honor in France, consensus in the Netherlands and contract in the United States [IRI 89, IRI 00, IRI 98]. The work of P. d'Iribarne has also been the target of some criticisms, such as the transposition of conclusions drawn from the observations of one case study to other companies [CAZ 00], overestimation of the consistency and rationality of national sets, with the author boiling down local peculiarities in ways of operating to a single logic. As is stressed by Chanlat [CHA 90], "more or less homogeneous, there are often companies within a company; above all, a company is marked, regardless of its size, by its complexity and its greater or lesser degree of cohesion". Similar to the studies carried out on cultural phenomena by other researchers, the limitation common to the works by Hofstede and d'Iribarne arises from the fact that they, like everybody, are prisoners of their own representations, as the view taken of the various cultures cannot be uncoupled from the cultural context.

National culture plays a crucial role in knowledge management, as is demonstrated by numerous studies which have looked at the impact of national culture of the implementation of this process in modern organizations [KIN 07b]. These studies have focused both on the links between actors' national cultures and the communication between those actors and on the influence of national culture on the methods of organization and management [KWO 09].

1.6.2. *Organizational culture*

Introduced by Pettigrew in 1979, the expression "organizational culture" is not subscribed to by everyone today, although the majority of authors agree as to its universality, its historical determination, its social construct and its establishment. Despite the wide variety of definitions for this concept put forward in the literature (see Table 1.8), the functionalist definition given by Schein [SCH 85, SCH 92, SCH 96, SCH 04a, SCH 04b] has attracted a consensus from a wide proportion of researchers such as Bélanger [BÉL 94], Calori and Sarnin [CAL 91], Levin [LEV 00] and de Montigny [DEM 06]. The fact that a consensus has been constructed around Schein's definition also appears to reflect the fact that researchers in organizational sciences have a preference for a functionalist approach to organizational culture.

Schein's definition has its roots in the basic hypotheses which many authors refer to by the terms "values", "norms" or "behavioral rules". Schein [SCH 04b] himself explains that the difference arises from the fact that "over time, values, norms and rules can be taken to be acquired, and therefore, transformed into fundamental hypotheses, which thus become non-negotiable". The members of a group thus come to be certain that their way of perceiving, thinking and feeling is the right way [SCH 04b]. Thus, outsiders who do not accept these suppositions are believed to be crazy or from another planet.

Authors	Definitions
Bate [BAT 84]	Organizational culture is a series of beliefs and hypotheses that are relatively widespread within the organization and are considered to be part of that organization by its members.
Schein [SCH 85, SCH 92, SCH 96, SCH 04a, SCH 04b]	Organizational culture is a set of basic hypotheses from which a group has learned that it is capable of solving problems of adaptation – both external and internal – and which has worked sufficiently well to be considered to be valid and be passed on to new arrivals as the correct way of perceiving, thinking and feeling in any relation to these problems.
Thévenet [THÉ 86]	Organizational culture includes anything which unifies the organization's practices, setting it apart from the others.
Bourdon [BOU 04a]	Organizational culture produces a system of rules and standards which guide individuals' behaviors.
de Montigny [DEM 06]	Organizational culture is a set of premises shared by the different members of the organization.

Table 1.8. *The main definitions of organizational culture*

In the view of King [KIN 07b], who refers to the integrationist approach to organizational culture put forward by Schein [SCH 85, SCH 92, SCH 04b], there exists only one culture within an organization: a culture made up of artifacts, values and basic hypotheses. The author identifies various levels of organizational culture likely to influence knowledge management in the organization. Thus, he distinguishes the organizational climate, the organizational subcultures, the unit cultures and the team climate:

– *Organizational climate* reflects a contextual situation at a given moment in time; it is linked to the individuals' behavior at that moment. The organizational culture includes multiple different organizational climates. Trust [HIN 03], openness and reasonable tolerance of failure [LEO 98] are important positive aspects of the organizational climate;

– *Organizational culture* can be considered to be a mixture of *subcultures*, each with its own basic hypotheses, its own values and its own artifacts. This is not incompatible with the integrationist view of organizational culture advanced by Schein. Organizational subcultures reflect the organization's structure, the professional occupations, the "ethical" values, the technologies used or the rank within the hierarchy;

– *Unit cultures* are specifically linked to the activity of an organizational unit, such as a department or a service. For example, the accounting department may have a departmental culture which is heavily impregnated by legal aspects. Organizational subcultures are generally different from unit cultures, because they do not refer to one particular unit, and generally transcend the boundaries of the organizational units;

– The *team climate*: a team is an organizational device that brings together the diverse specialized knowledge of multiple individuals in order to achieve a common goal [COO 01]. Often, a team is focused on a single objective and is short-lived; so, we use the term "team *climate*" rather than "team *culture*". If all the members of a team belong to the same organization, then the team climate, in part, reflects the organizational climate and culture.

1.6.3. *Professional culture*

The concepts of "occupation" and "profession" have been defined by multiple authors. Dubar and Tripier [DUB 03] define an occupation as representing simultaneously a job, a position and a set of people carrying out the same activity. Descolonges [DES 96], focusing closely on the issues of an occupation, ties together the concepts of work, oeuvre and action. According to Osty [OST 02], an occupation is a profession which also pertains to the construction of a common framework of judgement and a collective of belonging identifiable by its behavioral norms, its values or its representations. For Bucher and Strauss [BUC 92], Dieng *et al.* [DIE 00] and Osty [OST 02], a profession is a relatively homogeneous community whose members share an identity, values, definitions of the tasks and interests. Thus, the actors belonging to the same professional community are likely to present common behavioral norms and are linked by a certain amount of cognition peculiar to their profession [MON 08].

Practices, professional culture, identity, communities and groups of actors in the same profession have been studied in sociology of professions. They are all entities that are indicative of the "professional representations" uniting the ideas shared by the individuals about a given occupation [BLI 99]. Thus, Kwong and Levitt [KWO 09] analyzed the impact of national culture on the difference in decision-making when faced with an ethical problem, based on three samples of healthcare professionals in Saudi Arabia, Egypt and the United States. Between those healthcare professionals, the differences linked to national culture do not appear to play a significant role in terms of decision-making. This phenomenon can be explained by the narrowing of the cultural gap and a similarity of the models of thought, caused by a significant appropriation of their professional culture – particularly because of the standardization of medical training.

Certain authors have demonstrated that individuals' behaviors in the sharing and gathering of knowledge can be influenced by professional characteristics [MON 08].

The Design of the Learning Organization

In the first section of this chapter, we present the fundamentals of our theoretical model: the systematic approach and the organizational design.

In the second section, we discuss the construction of our research model in the domain of knowledge management.

2.1. From the systemic approach to the organizational design

As the analytical approach[1] appears to be insufficient to understand complex, fuzzy, changeable and imperfectly structured situations, which are often encountered in reality, in this chapter, we develop and then apply the systemic approach to organizational design.

2.1.1. *Systemic approach*

System theory [BER 68, BER 93] was developed to remedy the weaknesses of the analytical approach in dealing with complex situations.

We can present the systematic approach through the lens of a few major principles.

2.1.1.1. *Definition and characteristics of a system*

Numerous definitions of a system have been presented in the literature (see Table 2.1). In this book, we adopt the following generic definition: a system is a set of

---

1 The analytical approach has two important features. The first pertains to its objectives: to discover, explain, understand, predict and control reality. The second is its attempt at universality. For over 200 years, it has dominated western academic thought and is applied in all areas of human knowledge.

elements interacting with one another in accordance with a set of principles and rules. A system's characteristics will be of varying richness depending on its level of complexity. The model of nine levels of complexity of a system was presented by Kenneth E. Boulding in 1956. In 1985, the same author presented a second model of the hierarchy of systems, with 11 levels[2] (see Table 2.2). The nine-level model was taken up again by Bertalanffy [BER 68, BER 93] and Le Moigne [LEM 77].

Authors	Definitions
Leibniz [LEI 66]	A system is a set of parts.
De Saussure [SAU 31]	A system is an organized whole, made up of united elements which can only be defined in relation to one another, as a function of their place in the whole.
Von Bertalanffy [BER 68, BER 93]	A system is a complex of interacting elements.
Mélèze [MÉL 72]	With aims and goals being expressed in an environment, a finalized system is an organized collection of resources, methods, rules and procedures which are capable of obtaining satisfactory responses from the environment.
De Rosnay [DER 75]	A system is a set of elements interacting dynamically, organized with a view to a particular goal.
Le Moigne [LEM 77, LEM 90]	A system is an object which, in an environment, and having specific goals, carries out an activity and has its internal structure evolve over time, but without therefore losing its unique identity.
Morin [MOR 77]	A system is an inter-relating set of elements constituting an entity or an overall unity.
Checkland [CHE 81]	A system is a model of a whole entity; when applied to human activity, it is characterized in terms of hierarchical structure, emergent properties and communication and control networks. When applied to natural or manmade sets, the emergent properties that can be seen are the primary characteristic of a system.
Checkland [CHE 90]	A system is a complex set which may possess properties that are found in the whole system but are not meaningful or representative of the parts making up that system. These are known as emergent properties.

Table 2.1. *Definitions of a system*

2 Source: Wikipedia.

In the context of the issue discussed is this book, we situate ourselves at the level of a social system, which corresponds to level 8 in Boulding's 1956 model [BOU 56] and level 10 in his 1985 model [BOU 85]. In the next section of this chapter, we briefly present the main properties of a social system.

Level	1956 model	1985 model	Von Bertalanffy 1968 [BER 68]
1	Canvas	Mechanical system	Static structures
2	Clock	Kinematic system	Clocklike motions
3	Thermostat	Positive-feedback system	Self-regulation mechanisms
4	Cell	Creodic system	Open systems
5	Plant	Reproductive system	Low-level organisms
6	Animal	Demographic system	Animals
7	Human	Ecological system	Humans
8	Social organization	Evolutionary system	Sociocultural systems
9	Transcendental system	Human system	Symbolic systems
10		Social system	
11		Transcendental system	

Table 2.2. *Eleven-level hierarchy of systems*

2.1.1.2. *The properties of a social system*

The main properties of a social system are its goal, openness, complexity, equifinality and interaction.

2.1.1.2.1. Goal

It is difficult for social systems to function effectively and sustainably without goals. These goals must be determinant and must be known to the different actors.

At the same time, these goals must be able to evolve and adapt flexibly to the context. It even appears that the goal of a complex adaptive system is to be able to modify its own goals as a function of its environment and of the resources at its disposal. The goals of a social system may arise from within that system itself, from other systems or from the environment. Whether imposed or chosen with different degrees of freedom, they may be subject to a consensus, a compromise, divergences or "re-framing".

Social systems do not have the capability or the possibility of directly defining their goals, because it is the human operatives who establish the objectives. In addition, the objectives of social systems may be fuzzy, multiple and, sometimes, contradictory.

2.1.1.2.2. Openness

The openness of a system can be defined as its capacity to exchange energy, matter or information with other systems or with the environment. This property expresses the permanent relation and mutual influence between a system and its environment.

Thus, an organization evolves in different economic, competitive, social, legal (etc.) environments. Each of those environments is more or less hostile, stable or complex.

2.1.1.2.3. Complexity

The degree of complexity of a system depends on the number of its components and on the number and type of relations linking those components. Social systems are considered to be complex systems.

2.1.1.2.4. Equifinality

The principle of equifinality is stated as follows: "The same final state can be reached starting from different initial states, by different paths" [BER 68, p. 38]. Thus, there is no unique or exclusive solution to the problems encountered in open systems. This principle guided Miles and Snow [MIL 78] to design their theory of organizational configurations. According to these authors, companies in the same sector may adopt different strategies and obtain comparable results, on condition that their subsystems (entrepreneurial, technico-economic and administrative) are consistent. This condition touches on a final principle of system theory: that of the interaction of the components of a system.

2.1.2. *The "organizational design" school of thought*

The transposition of the systemic approach to organizations is relatively old: the work of Parsons [PAR 64], taken up again by Katz and Kahn [KAT 66], expounds upon the idea that the organization is a social system which has all the characteristics of an open system.

The founder of the organizational design school of thought, J.R. Galbraith [GAL 73], devised a model – called the "star model" – representing an organization as a set of five subsystems interacting with one another: strategy, rewards, human resources, processes and structure.

2.1.2.1. *The origin of Galbraith's "star model"*

Galbraith's star model [GAL 73] was preceded by Leavitt's "diamond" model [LEA 63], with which it has many points in common. Leavitt's model [LEA 63], inspired by the sociotechnical school, describes an organization as a system composed of the following elements: individuals, tasks, structure and technology for production of goods and services. Stohr and Konsynski [STO 92] enriched this model by adding a fifth component: information technology (IT) (see Figure 2.1).

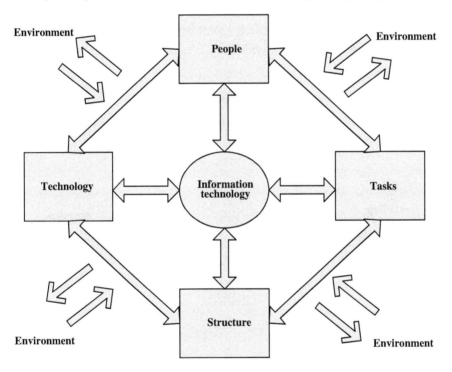

Figure 2.1. *Leavitt's model [STO 92]*

2.1.2.2. *Galbraith's "star model"*

On the basis of an initial work, very similar to the work of the organization behavioral school, and in line with Leavitt's model [LEA 63], J.R. Galbraith [GAL 73] developed a star-shaped model enabling directors to design organizational structures capable of effectively orienting organizational behavior. This so-called "star model" is a framework integrating different possible choices of design of organizations.

Galbraith [GAL 77] defines[3] organizational design as being "the search for coherence between the strategy (domain, objectives and goals), the mode of organization (division into subtasks, coordination to perform the totality of the tasks) and integration of people (selection and training of personnel, and design of a rewards system" [GAL 77, p. 5]. The domain relates to the activity performed by the organizational unit, which is usually a business unit of a group. The presentation of the star model [GAL 02b] is inspired by the author's most recent and most generic work (Figure 2.2).

Five domains of organizational design must be distinguished: strategy, incentive systems, staff policy, processes and structure.

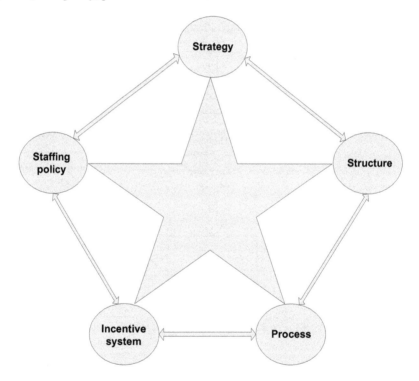

Figure 2.2. *Star model [GAL 02b]*

---

3 "[O]rganizational design is the search for coherence between strategy (domain, objectives and goals), organizing mode (decomposition into subtasks, coordination for completion of whole tasks) and integrating individuals (selection and training of people, designing a reward system" [GAL 77, p. 5].

2.1.2.2.1. Strategy

Strategy relates to the firm's vision of the future, its objectives, its values and its missions. It indicates the direction to be taken, specifying the products and/or services to be offered, the markets to target and the value to be provided to the customers. It determines the criteria used to select the appropriate organizational forms. In fact, each organizational form favors the performance of certain activities and inhibits that of others. The strategy identifies the fundamental activities and lays the groundwork for choosing organizational alternatives, which inevitably involve a degree of compromise.

2.1.2.2.2. Incentive systems

Incentive systems are aimed at bringing individuals' goals into line with those of the organization to which they belong. They provide the motivation necessary to go in the desired direction and carry out the company's strategy. They may relate to tangible aspects such as salaries, individual or collective bonuses, promotions, profit sharing or the awarding of shares to the employees. On the other hand, they may pertain to intangible aspects which give recognition of the individuals' contribution to the organization.

2.1.2.2.3. Staffing policies

Staffing policies pertain to recruitment, selection, internal mobility, training and development of people. These policies help to construct the capabilities needed to implement the strategy.

2.1.2.2.4. Processes

The processes relate to the design of integration or the means of coordination between organizational units. They give rise to informational and decisional flows which traverse the organizational structure vertically and horizontally. Vertical flows include allocation of resources and relate to the processes of planning and attribution of budgets. Horizontal flows represent transversal workflows: the development of a new product and the processing of the whole cycle of a customer order. The processes lend the organization flexibility by way of a network of interactions, enabling it to deal with all sorts of unforeseen problems. Four categories of processes, or means of integration of the organizational units, can be employed: coordination by informal groups, coordination by artifacts (information and communication technology (ICT)), creation of integrating manager positions and construction of a matricial organization. Each process entails its own advantages and disadvantages. The need for integration of the organizational units depends on five factors: their degree of interdependence, the diversity of the organization's activities, the instability of the environment, the ICT employed and the lifecycle of the products and/or services offered by the organization. The greater these factors are, the stronger will be the need for coordination, necessitating the use of complex and costly means of coordination which have the potential to cause conflict. Process design consists, first, of designing these means of integration of the units, taking account of the peculiarities of the organization (the contingency variables guiding the design of the strategy and structure which, themselves, will guide the design of the processes) and, second, of seeking coherence between these processes and the other components of the model (the people and incentive systems).

2.1.2.2.5. Structure

The structure relates to the design of the differentiation of the organizational units. It is designed with four parameters in mind: the specialization, the form, the power distribution and the services. To begin with, the specialization reflects the type and amount of specialized knowledge used to carry out the organization's activities. Next, the form pertains to the range of subordination at each level of the structure. The power distribution refers to the concepts of centralization and decentralization, in its vertical dimension and to the distribution of power pertaining to the tasks delegated to the organizational units (subsidiaries, business units, boards of directors and departments), in its lateral dimension. Finally, the services are constructed on the basis of the functions, the products, the markets, the geographic areas and the workflows.

The chosen design must integrate the criteria arising from the strategy and from the structure. The different facets of the organizational design must be harmoniously aligned with one another, so as to send a clear and consistent message to the company's employees. The model enables directors to influence the performance and culture by way of the different facets of the organizational design, with each structure bringing its own advantages and disadvantages. Once the structure has been chosen, it is possible to remedy its drawbacks by taking action on the other components of the design.

Drawing inspiration from the star model and basing our reasoning on the results of the work on knowledge management, we have created a model of a knowledge-oriented organization, which we call the "learning organization design". This model, which we shall now present, serves as a framework to define the topics where we are going to seek the conditions favoring and/or limiting the development of knowledge management in the organization.

2.2. Proposal of an organizational design for knowledge management: "learning organization design"

Today, research in the field of knowledge management is considered to be a true field of research in its own right, involving different disciplines of management:

strategy, human resources, information system, etc. However, the specificity of the research object studied in the publications on knowledge management has, for a long time, mobilized research and authors in a wide variety of other fields (psychology, computer science, mathematics, sociology, etc.), covering varied and sometimes-disjointed topics (knowledge management systems (KMSs), organizational learning, knowledge engineering, collaborative working tools, communities of practice, etc.). Before presenting our conceptual model, we shall offer an overview of the work recently published and currently under way in the domain of knowledge management. In particular, the aim here is to identify, within this domain, the major trends in current research likely to help elucidate our problem, with a view to studying the feasibility of integrating knowledge management at all levels of the organization. Our analysis of the conditions favoring and/or hampering the process of knowledge management in project teams is at the crossroads between these various theoretical schools of thought.

2.2.1. *Classification of works pertaining to knowledge management*

The research on knowledge management and the tools supporting it can be divided into five categories (I, II, III, IV and V), which indicate its disciplinary, theoretical and practical foundations. Our aim here is not to give an exhaustive presentation of these different schools of thought but, instead, to highlight certain elements which we feel are important for the problem at hand. Table 2.3 shows the different theories that can be used in the area of knowledge management: theories from which we ourselves drew inspiration when constructing our model.

I Seminal publications in knowledge management	II Organizational learning
[NON 95, DAV 98a, HAN 99, ALA 01, CAR 02a, CAR 03, CAR 04, CAR 05, HAN 07]	[POL 67, ARG 78, COH 90, ARG 00, CAR 03]
III Strategic management and RBV and KBV Innovation	IV Management of information systems
[PEN 59, BAR 91, ZAN 95, GRA 96b, TEE 97, CAR 03, CAR 04]	[MAR 88, ORL 92, SAM 94, SAM 05, KIN 06, KIN 07a]
V Knowledge management and cultures in organizations	
[SCH 85, IRI 89, CHA 90, HOF 90, SCH 92, IRI 98, TRO 98, IRI 00, SCH 04a, SCH 04b, KIN 06, KIN 07a]	

Table 2.3. *Classification of publications about knowledge management*

The founding works in knowledge management (I) have, since research in this area began, demonstrated the advantage of studying knowledge management by cross-referencing technical/IT and managerial viewpoints.

The publications on organizational learning (II) provide elements of analysis which are essential in understanding the learning dynamic and the specificity of the knowledge resource.

The works on strategic management and innovation (III) confirm that knowledge management is anchored in research on obtaining a sustainable competitive edge for organizations.

The articles and books on management of information systems (IV) are necessary to illuminate our issue, given that knowledge-management actions are often supported by IT.

The work on knowledge management and culture in organizations (V) not only illustrates the impact of different types of culture on knowledge management but also highlights a relationship of dependency between culture and knowledge management.

2.2.2. *The learning organization design*

Using this model of the learning organization [BEN 10a, BEN 10b], we shall now attempt to understand and explain the conditions for development of the knowledge resource by the interaction of the components of the organization: strategy, incentive systems, people, IT and structure.

We are stepping away from Galbraith's model [GAL 02b] for the following three reasons.

To begin with, we feel it is essential to distinguish the processes from the IT. Although Galbraith groups them together into a single component, in actual fact, they are two different constructs. The processes may be supported by KMSs, but in reality, these systems are an instantiation of the process. This distinction has already been drawn in the literature specifically devoted to enterprise resource planning and process management. In this book, wherever possible, the distinction is drawn between the tools and the means of coordination [STO 92, CLA 96]. In our model, the processes constitute a modality of the structure: coordination devices.

Then, we have grouped incentive systems and staffing policy together, the reason being that both of these constitute actionable variables in people management.

Finally, we have introduced the "people" variable into the model, covering the individuals' personal characteristics which might influence the development and sharing of knowledge. These characteristics are difficult to act upon – at least in the short term – for the company directors.

With this aim in mind, our model shows the organization in the form of a five-pointed star (Figure 2.3) representing its five components (strategy, incentive systems, people, IT and structure). These five components of the organization constitute the topics of the conceptual framework we use to examine our problem [BEN 10a, BEN 10b].

In the literature, for each component in the model, we sought out the conditions which could encourage and/or limit the development of the knowledge resource within the organization.

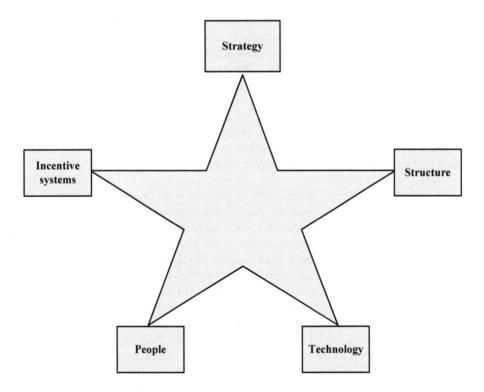

Figure 2.3. *The learning organization design*

2.2.2.1. *Strategy*

In 1959, Penrose noted the importance of knowledge in the economic system. She placed knowledge creation and learning capabilities at the center of the constitution and growth of firms. By attaching a financial value to knowledge, just like any other material asset, Penrose [PEN 59] opened the way for a new economic theory where knowledge is placed at the heart of the process of wealth creation [PER 06]. The firm thus appears to be a repertoire of knowledge where the services provided by those resources are contingent upon the experience and knowledge accumulated within the company. In the same vein, Ermine [ERM 03] postulates that knowledge constitutes a strategic issue, with his objectives of creation, capitalization and sharing of knowledge [PES 04]. Indeed, this capital, which has value, constitutes both a productivity factor and a durability factor for the company. The so-called "knowledge-based view" (KBV) school of thought sets the objective of organizational learning to better be able to transform knowledge into skills and reduce phenomena linked to opportunism and to the cognitive limitations of the actors engaged in a management situation [SAI 01]. The KBV school of thought is based on the observation that management processes consist of seeking out the means to manage, produce and disseminate knowledge, to generate collective skills by surpassing the intrinsic cognitive limitations, which leads to the distinction between individual knowledge and organization knowledge. Thus, organizational learning is the production and management of knowledge. This view is now becoming imposed as a dominant school of thought [GRA 96a], which is anchored in the resources and strategic skills "resource-based view" (RBV) school of thought. It postulates that knowledge – and especially tacit knowledge – is a resource that can serve as the source of a crucial competitive edge for the firm.

In order for knowledge management to succeed in an organization, knowledge management and its tools must be part of the organization's strategy, and the company's directors and managers must actively support that strategy. A knowledge-management strategy must lead to the identification of a target – that is the actors concerned, their needs, their sources of knowledge, the activities of the processes of knowledge management, the knowledge storage policy, the types of knowledge and the links between knowledge and KMS [MAN 98, GIN 99, SAG 99, HOL 00, KOS 01, JEN 03, YU 04]. A common structure of the knowledge at the scale of the whole organizational, clearly described and easily comprehensible, appears to be indispensable [DAV 98b, MAN 98, GIN 99, SAG 99, CRO 00, JEN 00, JEN 02]. The support of the organization's directors, including resource allocation and leadership, is a crucial factor in the success of projects in general, and especially projects to put knowledge management in place [DAV 98b, HOL 00, JEN 00, JEN 02, YU 04].

2.2.2.1.1. Knowledge management: a strategic objective

Numerous authors in the domain of knowledge management have highlighted the importance of creating an organizational climate that is favorable to knowledge-sharing activities [ODE 98, RUG 98, DAV 01]. Other authors point to the importance of having an environment where knowledge sharing is valued and is among the management's main concerns [MAN 98, GIN 99, SAG 99, HOL 00, MAR 00, KOS 01, MCD 01, JEN 03, YU 04].

2.2.2.1.2. Support from the company directors

The role of support from the organization's directors and managers in the success of knowledge management includes the allocation of resources, leadership and provision of training opportunities [DAV 98b, HOL 00, JEN 00, YU 04]. Management practices represent the opportunity for directors to influence the lives of their teams [BAR 04, BOU 04b]. Indeed, managerial actions are the best way to counteract an unfavorable context, or – on the other hand – to consolidate the lever which is a propitious situation for knowledge exchange and sharing [DUB 03]. The involvement of the general management in change and in new projects is often considered to be an important factor in the success of knowledge-management projects [KAL 05, KAL 07] and in the development of communities of practice [WEN 02]. In keeping with the existing literature, we consider managerial support to be a condition necessary for the development of knowledge.

2.2.2.2. *Incentive systems*

To bring personal goals into line with the organization's goals, the incentive systems employed in our model provide the necessary motivation to move in the desired direction and implement the company's strategy. Many authors believe that incentive systems and elements of staffing policy (such as training and integration devices) represent tools that are favorable to KM [DAV 98b, GIN 99, ALA 00, CRO 00, JEN 00, MAL 03, YU 04]. These systems may not only pertain to tangible aspects but also include intangible aspects arising from the staffing policy and the social climate.

2.2.2.2.1. Financial incentive systems

Mainly, financial incentive systems relate to salaries, individual and collectives bonuses and any type of tangible rewards [GAL 73, GAL 77, GAL 02b].

2.2.2.2.2. Non-financial incentive systems

The existing literature distinguishes the following non-financial incentive systems: training, organizational culture and trust.

– Training

Through awareness-raising and training devices, employees come to see and recognize the importance of knowledge management for the company [ALA 00].

Yet, this necessary condition is not a sufficient condition. Indeed, various authors have pointed out the importance of an organizational culture encouraging activities of contribution and knowledge sharing.

– Organizational culture

Numerous studies [DAV 98a, ODE 98, DEL 01, BHA 02] stress the importance of organizational culture of knowledge sharing and illustrate the relation between culture, on the one hand, and knowledge sharing and dissemination, on the other. Wenger *et al.* [WEN 02] estimate that culture can be a barrier to the development of links between the members of a community of practice. The KBV theory highlights the importance of taking the cultural aspect into account. O'Dell and Grayson [ODE 98] show that knowledge transfer and sharing can only take place if organizations create an environment favorable to such activities within a group. They point out that the main obstacles to collaboration and knowledge sharing are cultural in nature. Davenport and Prusak [DAV 98a] support this idea, stressing the importance of a culture which facilitates the exchange, transfer and use of knowledge. However, it should be noted that this organizational culture is very difficult to change [MCD 00]. In addition, the current state of research offers a precise conclusion about the relations between a culture of sharing and a culture of knowledge and learning [DAV 98a, MCD 00, BOU 04b]. A culture of sharing has a positive influence on knowledge sharing and learning [DAV 98b, SAG 99, ALA 00, JEN 00, YU 04]. A culture of knowledge constitutes one facet of the organizational culture; it motivates and helps the individuals to create, share and use knowledge for the benefit and success of the organization [OLI 06].

Organizational culture can be considered a crucial factor in the success of KM and organizational learning [JAN 03].

– Trust

The phenomenon of trust influences people's attitudes, their behavior and their performance at work [DIR 01].

There are two facets to trust: trust in colleagues [DAV 98a, PAU 04] and trust in the management and the hierarchy [REN 08]. Indeed, while, as a general rule, trust constitutes a condition for the effective working of the business world, it becomes absolutely necessary so that the people can contribute to knowledge management without fear of being, first, dispossessed of their *savoir-faire* and, second, made redundant.

– Trust in colleagues

Many researchers in the area of knowledge management – particularly Roberts [ROB 00], Rolland and Chauvel [ROL 00] and Davenport and Prusak [DAV 98a] – believe that trust is an essential condition for any exchange of knowledge – especially online [GOU 04, PAU 04, PRA 07]. Thus, Connelly and Kelloway [CON 00] consider that an individual will only share his/her knowledge with individuals whom he/she trusts. According to Paul and McDaniel [PAU 04], trust is necessary for a collaborative relationship to be maintained. The greater the degree of trust, the more willing the person is to share his/her information and knowledge. Okhuysen and Eisenhardt [OKH 02] and Van Baalen *et al.* [VAN 05] hold lack of trust to be a barrier to socialization and learning. For their part, Muller and Carey [MUL 02] state that lack of trust between groups can constitute a key barrier to knowledge-sharing activities. In a similar vein of ideas, Charbit and Fernandez [CHA 03] emphasize trust as a necessary condition for knowledge sharing. Baillette and Lebraty [BAI 02b, p. 134] analyze the role played by trust in the success of collaborative work: "Trust stems from a cycle of exchanges, punctuated by giving and counter-giving between actors who are both free and constrained at the same time. It refers to a belief which manifests itself in two dimensions linked to "moral" aspects: a belief in the fact that the other party (or parties) has/have good intentions towards us, and a "technical" belief in the fact that our interlocutor has the skills we expect of him/her".

In an atmosphere of trust, of "psychological security", it is possible for the members of a team to take inter-personal risks [EDM 99]. This atmosphere of psychological security has a positive influence on the sharing and learning behaviors of the team members, which favorably affects the team's performance.

Thus, a climate of trust within a team, between colleagues, is a condition favoring the behavior of knowledge sharing and learning and constitutes a condition for the development of knowledge in the organization [BAI 02c].

– Trust in the management

In the 1960s, Argyris [ARG 64] noted that trust in the management is important for the organizational performance. Trust in the management produces higher levels of cooperation and knowledge sharing, which ultimately improves the performance. Trust increases individuals' motivation to share their knowledge [MAY 95]. Trusting relationships lead to more knowledge exchanges [DIR 01]. Levin and Cross [LEV 04] suggest that this cooperation between individuals is crucial to knowledge sharing. Interpersonal knowledge sharing and exchange of experiences is more likely to happen in trusting relationships [DOD 93]. Other studies have pointed to the significant influence of trust in the management on results and performance [ARG 64, ZAH 98, DIR 00]. By analyzing knowledge sharing within and between the teams in an organization, Renzl [REN 08] studied the influence of trust in the hierarchy. He characterizes that trust by the lack of worry about losing one's possessed knowledge and by an increased motivation to document one's own personal knowledge.

In our research, we shall take account of this double facet of trust, in colleagues and in the management.

2.2.2.3. *People*

People act within a structure by using different coordination devices and tools. However, their behavior, guided by incentive systems toward the realization of the strategic aims, is not completely determined. A person's age, gender, previous experience, hierarchical level occupied, mastery of spoken and written language and the national culture are the main individual characteristics identified in the literature as being able to influence the development of the knowledge resource within the organization, and we have used these characteristics in construction of our research model.

2.2.2.3.1. Age

Considered by Jarvenpaa and Staples [JAR 01] to be a dimension which influences the adoption of knowledge-sharing behavior, age seems to be a factor which is likely to influence behaviors of knowledge sharing and contribution within a group or a team. The younger a person is, the more they share, and the more inclined they are to make use of ICT.

2.2.2.3.2. Gender

Gender is considered by Jarvenpaa and Staples [JAR 01] as a characteristic which could influence a person's attitude and behavior toward sharing. Women are more likely than men to adopt knowledge-sharing attitudes and behaviors [BOU 04a]. Tremblay's research [TRE 05] shows that women integrate into the learning model very well.

2.2.2.3.3. Previous experience of sharing and knowledge exchange

Prior experience of sharing, exchange and use KM tools can constitute a condition for the development of knowledge within a group. Case studies by CEFRIO [CEF 05] show the usefulness of experience in sharing activities. These works demonstrate that, if the members of a team are new to the field, they may have little or no previous experience of sharing. The team's sharing experience may be middling or even significant if its members are already part of a formal or informal network and have already played a role in other working teams.

2.2.2.3.4. Hierarchical level

The individual's hierarchical level may also constitute a condition on the development of knowledge. The higher a person's grade is, the more confident he/she will be in his/her knowledge, and thus he/she will be more willing to share that knowledge. We believe that this condition could influence knowledge-sharing behavior, as did Constant *et al.* [CON 94]. Jarvenpaa and Staples [JAR 01] deem that the higher up a person is, the more he/she will value knowledge sharing.

2.2.2.3.5. Language

A person's mother-tongue is also a condition which could influence the development of knowledge in the organization. In a context similar to that of the project team, Wenger *et al.* [WEN 02] consider written language to be a barrier to the development of a community of practice, in that the tool, created to support exchanges between the participants, inevitably requires that they express themselves in writing. Indeed, certain people may be fearful of written communication, because they feel their level of command of the written language is poorer than the rest of the team members. Although the results in this domain are sometimes contradictory, certain authors have shown that some individuals systematically avoided situations where they would have to write [DAL 75, DWY 98, cited in DUB 04].

2.2.2.3.6. National culture

Numerous studies show the impact of national culture on the communication between actors and on the methods of organization and management – aspects which are crucial to take into account in the context of our research. In the context of dominant oral culture, it is hard to expect formal and structured information. "How can we use written procedures when to use them may be perceived as communicating a lack of trust?" asks Barzantny [BAR 02]. The idea that the medium is the message [MCL 72] can be applied to ICT. This technology, which facilitates new kinds of organization such as virtual teams, generally does not take account of the peculiarities of national culture. For example, in Maghrebi culture, face-to-face communication is hugely important, and the locals are particularly reticent to adopt remote communication methods such as telephone, fax, e-mail or video-conferencing, whereas for Americans, the practice of long-distance communication poses no problem [BAR 06].

The legitimacy of the modes of organization and management differs considerably depending on the cultural context. Although paternalism is a thing of the past in certain western countries, in many others, it continues to be a guiding framework. For example, in Asian countries, the boss encourages, protects, assumes his/her share of responsibility in case of a mistake or misdeed by an employee and devotes a great deal of time to social events. In Asia, subordinates display a great deal of reverence toward their superiors. In view of the importance of God in

African culture, Africa is also a favorable context for paternalism, according to Etounga [ETO 91]. Assimilated to divine will, power and authority must be demonstrated and exercised and not shared.

In the countries of the Maghreb, subordinates conduct exchanges with their superiors on an equal footing; for instance, managers wait in the same queue as everyone else in the company canteen. According to d'Iribarne [IRI 98], "their expectations of equality are concentrated in a symbolic register, and overlook power sharing".

2.2.2.4. Technology: KMS

In the views of many authors [ORL 92, ALA 01, RUB 01], knowledge management is not based solely on the development and use of a tool [MCD 99, BOU 04a]. That tool must possess functions which are useful and are perceived as such by the users; otherwise, the technology may lead a community to stray from their path, and the KM project to failure [BAN 03]. In addition, as is shown by the works of DeSanctis and Poole [DES 94] and of DeSanctis et al. [DES 03], the characteristics of a KMS may alter the approaches and working processes of a group [BEN 15a].

The choice of KMS tools must take account of various characteristics, such as ergonomics, ease of use, friendliness and perceived usefulness, as these factors are likely to influence users' behavior when using the tool [DAV 89]. In terms of knowledge management, the ease of creation, dissemination, memorization, finding and updating of the knowledge are factors which influence usage behaviors [GOO 98].

The *Technology Acceptance Model* (TAM) was developed by Davis [DAV 89] to study and explain the acceptance and use of IT. The purpose of the model is to determine the impact of external factors on an individual's internal beliefs, attitudes and behavior. Davis identified a number of fundamental variables suggested by previous studies on the cognitive and affective determining factors for technology acceptance. He then used the theory of reasoned action as a theoretical basis to specify the causal relations between the identified variables. The model explains the user's attitude, his/her intentions and behavior toward the adoption of computer technologies in light of their perceived usefulness (PU) and perceived ease of use (PEOU). Thus, the TAM can explain [STR 97] and predict the success or failure of the adoption of new technologies. If we know, *a priori*, the determining factors for the acceptance of a system, it should be possible to anticipate the changes needing to be made in order for that system to be accepted [TAY 95].

2.2.2.4.1. Perceived usefulness

PU is "the degree to which a person believes that using a particular system would enhance his or her job performance" within the organization [DAV 89]. This construct is a theoretical substitute for the concept of *relative advantage* developed in technology adoption theory [CHI 01]. The relative advantage to a technology is evaluated by comparison with the technology which it is intended to supplant. It may arise in the form of financial profit, social prestige or another form of benefit [ROG 95]. In the context of our research, PU denotes the advantages that the individual thinks s/he can derive from using KMS tools to facilitate his/her task. The advantages anticipated from using the tool, such as a time gain, money or any other expected advantage, positively influence users' attitude toward the adoption of the tool in question.

2.2.2.4.2. Perceived ease of use

The PEOU is "the degree to which a person believes that using a particular system would be free from effort" [DAV 89]. In the view of Vogel *et al.* [VOG 01], "it is important, to support a group working remotely, to strike the right balance between functions and ease of use". In virtual or partially virtual groups, technological problems may actually give rise to interaction problems. Too high a number of functions can lead to excess complexity of use, which can throw off an inexperienced user. Moreover, as mentioned by McDermott [MCD 00], in addition to ease of use in itself, we need to include the way in which the tool integrates into the actor's work – particularly with the pre-existing tools. The easier the technology is to access, the greater will be its positive impact on the members' participation, learning and satisfaction. Dubé [DUB 04, p. 27] suggests that: "if a user presses 'enter' and the system takes a few seconds[4] before responding, this may negatively influence his use and therefore his participation".

Ease of use has a positive impact on members' participation, learning and satisfaction [DUB 04]. In the literature on information systems, the PEOU positively influences the use of the information system [DAV 89]. Other research in information systems has confirmed this result [MOO 91, TAY 95, ADA 92, VEN 99]. In terms of knowledge management, the ease of creation, dissemination, memorization, finding and updating of the knowledge influences the behavior of use of KMSs [GOO 98].

2.2.2.4.3. Perceived consequences

According to Triandis [TRI 80], individuals behave differently depending on the degree of certitude with which they perceive the potential consequences, whether positive or negative, of their acts. Thompson *et al.* [THO 91] respectively speak of expected consequences and of expected results. If the perceived consequences are positive, then the attitude toward the adoption of KMSs will be favorable.

---

4 An IBM study demonstrated, when the first transactional information systems were installed (1980), that the ideal response time – i.e. that which would not cause a drop in productivity – should be less than 2 seconds.

2.2.2.5. *Structure of the company*

Various structural characteristics are likely to favor or limit the development of the knowledge resource in the organization: the number of hierarchical levels within the organization, autonomy, interdependence of tasks, mutual adjustment and professional characteristics.

2.2.2.5.1. Number of hierarchical levels

Usually, a very hierarchical structure limits individuals' autonomy. Indeed, the bureaucratic structure involves numerous rules and procedures which govern everyone's work. Such a structure, therefore, is not favorable to the development and sharing of knowledge. The more hierarchical levels there are, the less inclined people are to share their knowledge [COH 97].

2.2.2.5.2. Autonomy

Autonomy may be defined as the extent to which people and/or teams have a certain amount of freedom in the choice of different aspects of their activity: methods and means of work, deadlines, objectives in terms of results, etc. The higher the degree of autonomy, the less control is imposed from the outside. Teams with a high level of autonomy decide on how to carry out the tasks and what needs to be done. Thus, they are responsible for their own learning behavior and knowledge sharing. It is the members of the team, rather than the supervisors, who make the decisions and organize the work processes. In accepting that responsibility, the team members will implement all their resources, including their knowledge and skills, in order to obtain the desired objectives and results. This does not preclude the presence of a team leader, who can, in fact, improve the team's capacity for autonomy [STE 00].

2.2.2.5.3. Interdependence of tasks

Thompson [THO 67] distinguished three types of interdependence: interdependence of pooled tasks, sequential interdependence of tasks and reciprocal interdependence of tasks.

– Interdependence of pooled tasks: Collaborators perform their tasks independently of one another. There is little need for direct contact. Such is the case, for example, with daytime and night-time shifts on a production line or with franchised restaurants. Very little coordination seems necessary, and rules and procedures can be established for the coordination of routine tasks.

– Sequential interdependence of tasks: The performance of the tasks requires more planning. The upstream terminal must have finished its work before the downstream terminal can begin working. Such is the case, for instance, with the building of a house: we cannot build the roof until the foundations have been laid and the walls built.

– Reciprocal interdependence of tasks: Information exchanges between the collaborators are necessary during the fulfillment of their respective tasks. In a restaurant, the kitchen staff depends on the front-of-house staff to bring them the orders, but the waiting staffs are also dependent upon the kitchen staff to serve the meal and satisfy the customer.

Because it is impossible to predict everything, the rules are never fully complete. In addition, the actors may seek to develop or maintain relative autonomy. These two major reasons mean that coordination by information systems is dependent on the actors' attitudes – cooperative or otherwise [DET 92].

The exact definition of "cooperation" is difficult to pin down. Chen *et al.* [CHE 98] distinguish six elements whereby cooperation is obtained:

1. Super-goal: when the individual goals are incompatible, the reference to a super-goal helps to move past the conflicts [TJO 84].

2. Collective identity: the ability to recognize oneself as forming part of a group.

3. Trust.

4. Empowerment, which manifests itself by the acceptance of control devices.

5. Communication, which improves cooperation when it is more intense.

6. Structure of incentive systems.

The two concepts of interdependence and cooperation, therefore, need to be distinguished. Groups whose members are interdependent and work cooperatively perform better [WAG 95]. The quality of the cooperation in a team is an important factor in the success of innovations [COO 93, NON 95].

Interdependencies of knowledge are denoted by the term "shared interest" by Fillol [FIL 06]. From our point of view, interdependence of the tasks in the process of knowledge management involves, though not exclusively, at least a few elements of cooperation (the trust, the incentive system).

2.2.2.5.4. Working processes

On the basis of this topic, we seek to understand how the working processes can be favorable to the development of knowledge – particularly if they include the gathering, sharing and use of knowledge [CRO 00, JEN 00]. The two occupational processes in our field of research are described precisely in Chapter 3.

2.2.2.5.5. Mutual adjustment: human contact

Mutual adjustment (face to face) often constitutes a coordination mechanism that is favorable to knowledge transfer [ODE 98]. Indeed, trust tends to develop more easily in face-to-face relations [MAR 01]. Tools offer no substitute for meetings in the flesh, which must still take place in order to build the mutual familiarity and trust necessary for future interactions.

In the eyes of H. Mintzberg [MIN 82], mutual adjustment consists of coordinating with one another informally, usually in face-to-face relations. Lack of human contact, of relations and of shared vision between the members of a team acts as a barrier to knowledge transfer [ODE 98]. In that sense, Markus [MAR 01] and Barrett *et al.* [BAR 04] stress that trust primarily develops in face-to-face relations. Other authors point out that ICT is no substitute for face-to-face meetings [DEL 01, SHA 97] and that such meetings must continue in order to construct mutual knowledge and the trust necessary for future interactions [BOU 04b].

2.2.2.5.6. Professional characteristics

The actors belonging to the same professional community are likely to exhibit shared behavioral norms and are linked by a certain number of ideas specific to their profession, according to Monnier [MON 08]. The practices, culture and identity of actors in the same profession have been studied in sociology of professions. It is entities indicative of the "professional representations" which represent all the ideas shared by the individuals about their occupation [BLI 99]. The individuals' behavior in terms of sharing and collecting knowledge can be influenced by the professional characteristics. Professional characteristics can account for the differences in behavior in knowledge sharing (deliberate capitalization upon and consultation of the KMS), between auditors, lawyers and consultants [MON 08]. The author demonstrated these differences by a comparative analysis of these three occupations in a large consultancy firm. The analysis was performed using the following eight significant variables: the form of the teamwork, the frequency of travel for work, the timeframe of the missions, the size of the population in the organization, the existence of a working methodology, the existence of a professional regulation code, the existence of alternatives to KMS and the existence of a dedicated piece of software for the occupation). The study shows behavioral differences in the use of the same KMS depending on the occupation: low consultation and capitalization on the KMS for the auditors, who preferred to exchange with the members of their team; a preference for paper documentation for lawyers, coupled with a certain individualism which runs counter to the disposition to share; and a more significant approach of sharing with consultants, both by the use of the KMS and by direct exchanges between colleagues.

Table 2.4 recaps all of the factors that we have identified in the literature which have an impact on the development of knowledge management (favoring and/or limiting it).

Components & Sources	Factors favoring and/or limiting knowledge management
Strategy O'Dell and Grayson [ODE 98], Davenport *et al.* [DAV 98b], Holsapple *et al.* [HOL 00], Jennex and Olfman [JEN 00]	KM: Strategic objective Support of the directors for KM
Incentive systems Galbraith [GAL, 73, GAL 77, GAL 02b], Davenport *et al.* [DAV 98b], Davenport and Prusak [DAV 98a], O'Dell and Grayson [ODE 98] Eisenhardt [EIS 89b], Prax [PRA 00], Argyris and Schön [ARG 02], Renzl [REN 08]	**Financial or tangible** Salary, bonus, promotion **Non-financial** Training Organizational culture Trust in their colleagues Trust in the management
People Jarvenpaa and Staples [JAR 00], Tremblay [TRE 05], Constant *et al.* [CON 94], Wenger *et al.* [WEN 02], Hofstede [HOF 80], d'Iribarne *et al.* [IRI 98]	Age Gender Training Experience Language National culture Hierarchical level
Technology DeSanctis and Poole [DES 94], Davis [DAV 89], O'Dell and Grayson [ODE 98], Markus [MAR 01], Alavi and Leidner [ALA 01]	Functions Use characteristics Perceived usefulness Ease of use Perceived results
Structure Cohen and Baily [COH 97], Stewart and Barrick [STE 00], Thompson [THO 67], Tjosvold [TJO 84], De Terssac [DET 92], Markus [MAR 01], Monnier [MON 08]	Number of hierarchical levels Autonomy Interdependence Cooperation Mutual adjustment Professional characteristics

Table 2.4. *Recap of the factors cited in the literature review*

Part 2

Emergence of a New Design: that of the Learning Organization

3

Real-World Access Methodology

The second part of this book aims to provide an answer to our questions, by way of an empirical study. Indeed, the construction of the conceptual framework and empirical analysis are two processes that are closely linked. The stitching together of the theoretical developments into a conceptual framework creates a frame of reference, which partly guides the collection and analysis of data. At the same time, the methodology employs conditions of the validity and reliability of the answers to our questions.

In section 3.1, we present the various methodological choices made in conducting this study.

In section 3.2, we present the field of research and its various evolutions. Indeed, our cross-cutting study has been able to track the significant organizational changes and radical restructurings of a merger between two worldwide telecoms groups.

In section 3.3, we outline the data-collection method.

To conclude, in section 3.4, we describe the resources deployed for the processing of the data collected.

Overall, the approach can be presented in this order, even though, in reality, there was a certain amount of to-ing and fro-ing between the different stages. As pointed out by Royer and Zarlowski [ROY 99], the search process is highly iterative, and the boundaries between the various stages tend to become blurred. The different activities (literature review, data collection and processing and analyses) are carried out in parallel, with the research focusing more attention on one or another of these activities at any one time [SEL 77].

3.1. Methodological choices

A researcher's choices are guided by their desire for consistency between the issue at hand, the research questions and the real-world access strategy. Here, we seek to identify the conditions for developing effective knowledge management (KM) in terms of learning and sharing between the members of a project team. The objective is to describe, understand and explain the dynamics of this kind of behavior. This investigation into the emergence of an organizational design that is effective for KM – which is partly exploratory – requires a qualitative method based on a case study. On the one hand, the way in which we view the reality studied here will define and justify the choices made as to the method of managing and formatting the results. On the other hand, that reality will lead us to define the approach taken to going into the field.

3.1.1. *Methodology*

In this section, we explain the relevance of the qualitative approach chosen and more specifically the choice of a cross-cutting approach based on a case study. The reasons behind those choices are explained in relation to the issue at hand and the researcher's position on the ground.

3.1.1.1. *Choice of a qualitative, cross-cutting approach*

Numerous researchers in organizational sciences advocate a qualitative and cross-cutting approach when aiming to understand the dynamics of a phenomenon [VAN 90, KOE 94]. They stress that these methods help to determine how a phenomenon arises, how it develops and how it takes root over time. According to Grawitz [GRA 93], qualitative methods allow us to describe, understand and explain processes anchored in a local and specific context. They also afford us the opportunity to collect data which are difficult to find by a quantitative approach [YIN 89]. Finally, in the view of Miles and Huberman [MIL 91], the qualitative approach provides rich descriptions and explanations, rooted solidly in processes embedded in a local context. Although a criticism of qualitative research is that it can lead to subjectivity on the part of the researcher, it does have the advantage of endowing the study with a certain amount of depth, in that the researcher is physically and psychologically close to the phenomenon they are observing.

3.1.1.2. *Use of a case study: a strategy for gaining real-world data*

The method chosen for this in-depth examination of the interactions between actors is based on a case study, which is a widely used research method, employed in the social sciences, and particularly in analyzing organizations and management [YIN 94]. According to Bonoma [BON 85], "a case study is a description obtained directly from a managerial situation, on the basis of interviews, archives, observations or any other information source, constructed to give an account of the situational context in which the phenomenon occurs". On the other hand, for Yin [YIN 89], it is "an empirical study which investigates a contemporary phenomenon in its real context, when the boundaries between the phenomenon and its context are not clearly apparent, and when multiple sources of proof are used". A case study is a research strategy that is particularly well suited when the research questions are of the type "how", "what" and "why", when the events under examination are contemporary and when it is not necessary to be able to control them. This corresponds well to the situation in which we find ourselves here: we seek to understand and explain "how" certain conditions in an organization can favor and/or limit KM in a project team. As this research is exploratory, there are no predefined propositions, but there is an objective: to understand and explain the process. Case studies are particularly recommended when venturing into new and complex fields, where there is little background theory available and where it is crucial to take account of the context to develop the process of comprehension. Yin [YIN 89] distinguishes four possible designs for a case study, depending on whether we choose to study one or several cases and use one or more analytical units or subunits within those cases. The design chosen in this instance is that of a single case study.

3.1.2. *Participant observation*

As the goal here is to understand and explain the conditions favoring and/or hampering KM in terms of learning and sharing between the organizational actors within a project team, we have chosen to present participant observation which offers a good understanding of the field, rich dialog with the different players involved and privileged access to a certain amount of data.

3.1.2.1. *Definition of participant observation*

According to Mucchielli [MUC 96, p. 146] "participant observation consists of actually participating in the lives and activities of the subjects one is observing, depending on the age, gender or status category the researcher manages to integrate him/herself into by negotiation with his/her hosts, based on the researcher's own desiderata, or the place the hosts agree to allow him/her to occupy". It is possible to distinguish four postures of a researcher on the ground ([BAU 99], based on [JUN 60] and [GOL 69]). The researcher may be a complete participant, a participant observer, an observer who participates or a complete observer.

3.1.2.1.1. The complete participant

As a complete participant, the researcher does not tell his/her subjects that s/he is a researcher. The observation is hidden, which in itself gives rise to significant ethical problems.

3.1.2.1.2. The participant observer

As a participant observer, the researcher has more freedom to carry out his/her investigations but is not in a neutral position in relation to his/her subjects. The other actors in the organization are aware of the researcher's double role, meaning they can more easily be consulted and so the researcher has access to a vast mass of data – both primary (participation in numerous meetings, formal and informal interactions) and secondary (project notes, confidential notes, freer access, etc.). However, in this position, it is not possible to reconcile the responsibilities of working in the organization and the work of research. In addition, a researcher who is a member of the organization will have difficulty in viewing the data objectively.

3.1.2.1.3. The observer who participates

As an observer who participates, the researcher has a marginal degree of participation in the life of the organization. The establishment of the relation of trust with his/her subjects provides access to rich and varied data. However, it is important, in this case, to make sure to maintain a neutral position in relation to the subjects. It is this position which was adopted during our research (although the length of our stay in the organization has led to the combination of several approaches). In terms of the difficulties mentioned further, we feel that this position allows a greater deal of latitude to conduct the research. We seek to understand and explain the conditions favoring and/or hampering KM in the organization, by analyzing the interactions between actors. Hence, we must have access to the inner circle of the organization, in order to be able to grasp its richness and complexity. There is no secrecy about our capacity as researchers. Our role in the workings of the organization was sporadic and peripheral but, nonetheless, helped to legitimize our presence on the site for several days a week over the course of 12 months.

3.1.2.1.4. The complete observer

As a complete observer, the researcher observes the terrain in a more-or-less systematic way, retaining an external perspective. Thus, during the study at hand, he/she is able to observe various factors which supplemented his/her understanding of the field (arrangement of premises, computing equipment, KM tools, training center, meeting spaces, individual behavior, etc.).

3.1.2.2. *The advantage to and difficulties with the position of "participant observation"*

As a participant observer, the researcher has access to various forms of data and allows him/her to attend meetings, committees and fora more naturally than by being just a simple observer. Wacheux [WAC 96] points out that "mere presence on site does not ensure the phenomenon will be observed. The researcher must be accepted by the group and be present at the opportune moments. With this in mind, participation in a mission favors presence and involvement". A researcher's experiences on the ground tends to validate this assertion. They seek to justify their presence in the teams. For instance, they could offer to take care of the writing and distribution of reports in training sessions *"Task force, Factory TM*, etc." They could also participate in various workshops, help in the development of various tasks such as the modeling of certain internal procedures and the drafting of their specifications, etc. This will be well received by certain members. Thus, a researcher will be able to able to gain access to numerous pieces of information, with a greater degree of flexibility and ease.

More generally speaking, the approach of participant observation seems of particular interest in the current context. Indeed, it allows access to very rich and detailed data and enables the researcher to be present on the ground at opportune moments and to help the actors on occasional points. In the context of shared trust, the researcher can remain in the background in relation to the normal workflow of the individuals in the organization, which is much more difficult in the case of the participant observer.

However, this approach is not easy to implement. For each of the aforementioned statuses, Gould [GOU 69] identified tensions between the roles of observer and researcher. In particular, the participant who observes, because of his/her proximity to the people under observation, is liable to adopt their point of view. On the other hand, the observer who participates risks remaining on the fringes of the observed group. Thus, Groleau [GRO 03] notes that over the course of her research, "it was difficult to strike a balance between the desire to constantly question our subjects in order to extend or validate our understanding, and the necessary restraint so as not to obstruct the subjects in the discharge of their daily duties by questioning them".

3.2. The field of research

The empirical research presented herein is based on a case study in a company belonging to the telecom sector.

We shall begin by presenting the research area and the different stages of the company's restructuring, changing from S Communication Competences Center (SCCC) to NSN CCC, whilst describing the context of the merger whereby one structure was transformed into another.

We will then explore the main occupations within the company, the operational activities and the way in which they come together to form processes, thus enabling projects to be carried out.

3.2.1. *Presentation of the research area*

The choice of research area was not made at random. To begin with, as the name indicates, "S Communication Competences Center" is a true crucible for the creation and development of competences and, therefore, knowledge, which was the first reason for the choice. Next, the second reason is the interest shown by the management of SCCC in this study and their proposal to explore the area more fully, granting total access.

3.2.1.1. *S Communication Competences Center*

SCCC is the research area into which the author initially entered. In light of unforeseen circumstances, a joint venture with the company N in the telecom domain transformed the initial terrain. Before describing the new structure, we shall present the multinational S to which the competences center belongs.

3.2.1.1.1. The enterprise S: history and implantation in Tunisia

S is an international corporate group. It is synonymous with innovation and sustainable development in sectors as diverse as IT and communications, energy and lighting, industrial processes, medicine and transport. Today, its activity relies on over 400,000 collaborators, millions of customers and hundreds of thousands of suppliers and partners in around 190 countries around the world. S has been present in Tunisia since 1932, first working with "H R & Co.", and then an electricity import and electrical work firm since 1953, which created TGM, the light metro in Tunis and the Sousse thermal power plant. It was only in the 1990s that the Group S made its first concrete investment in Tunisia, setting up the public limited company *Entreprise Tunisienne de Télécommunications ATEA-S* (ETTAS), following the signing of a partnership agreement with the Tunisian Ministry of Communication Technologies. ETTAS, which plays an active role in all the key activities of S International, notably specializes in the domain of telecommunications, where it has carried out large-scale switching and transmission projects on behalf of Tunisie Télécom. In 1995, the company decided to branch out. It developed a second branch of activity as the integrator of IT solutions essentially oriented toward communications and, along with Tunisian partners, put in place distribution networks for mobile stations and the computer products F S Computers. It was not until October 1, 1999 that ETTAS became a subsidiary belonging entirely to the parent company S, becoming S Information and Communications. From the earliest days, S Information and Communications built itself a solid reputation in Tunisia and abroad, as a center of expertise – especially for training of clientele. The technical, pedagogical and linguistic qualities of the Tunisian engineers, which are appreciated by customers in the region, enabled the company to export its skills and found the training center for the region of Africa and the Middle East, "S Communication Competences Center", in Tunis in 1998.

3.2.1.1.2. S Communication Competences Center (SCCC)

In 1998, S placed all of its training activities in an offshore company called S Communication Training Center in order to cater for a significant demand from international customers.

In 2001, the company was extended to form SCCC, integrating the activities of bid management and solution management, databases and engineering.

In 2002, a regional technical assistance center was set up. In 2003, the activities of technical and commercial project management were established. Between 2005 and 2007, SCCC served as an essential link in these activities for the group S regionally. That center is the offshore part of S in Tunisia, as opposed to the local company, called *S Tunisie*, which represents the onshore part. The objective of SCCC was not primarily financial; it was more of a cost center than a profit center (apart from the training center, which, in part, was able to generate profit). SCCC is concerned solely with the activity of Communication, which represents 95% of S's activity in Tunisia. This center was established by the parent company, which owns it entirely, with a view to delocalizing certain activities in Tunisia and better catering for an increasing demand from the Middle East and French-speaking Africa. An international team formed around a project, the majority of whom were in Tunis or in Munich, and some elsewhere in the world. All the members contributed with their own expertise in the area of the service to which they belonged. That team collaborated in the context of a project before and after the signing of the contract, until the project was concluded and the customer finally satisfied (with training and high-level technical support).

The way in which SCCC works is based on a structure composed of the following services and departments:

– *Technical Bid Management (TBM)*: management of the technical part of a bid;

– *Engineering*: detailed study before delivery, and the planning part of a network in general;

– *Project Management*: after the signing of the contract, this service takes care of the implementation of the project – that is relaying of the order, monitoring and management of the project in general;

– *Bid Management*: management of the technical and commercial part of a bid, coordination of a team (sometimes international) in the process of preparation of a bid.

– *Outside Plant*: implementation in the form of installation of communication stations and fiber-optic cables, etc. This service is comparable to that of TBM but for a specific technology, which pertains to external cabling, etc.;

– *Training Institute*: the training center for the engineers of S and its customers;

– *Remote Network Care Center (RNCC)*: the high-level technical support for maintenance groups. This service has its own information system which is connected to the center in Portugal.

3.2.1.2. *The context of the merger between the two companies S and N*

"Concentrations are continuing in the telecom sector. After the marriage of the two companies A and L, it is N and S's turn to merge their activities supplying mobile telephony and networking, in a co-enterprise known as NSN.

Each partner will hold 50% of the new structure, which is anticipated to save them €1.5b each year between now and 2010 (…). The operation should be finalized by 1 January 2007, after approval by the regulatory authorities. The two partners state that 'Based on the current data on market share, this will be the second-largest company in the world for mobile infrastructure and services, and the third-largest in the world in terms of fixed infrastructure and global telecom infrastructure'. The entity will be headed by the current Vice-President in charge of the networking branch at N. It will be the number 3 world supplier of telecom equipment, behind A/L and C." *La Presse* newspaper

A *joint venture* (JV) is an association whereby at least two people or entities come together in a variety of ways, to carry out a particular project, by pooling their knowledge, technologies and resources and sharing the risks and benefits. The potential advantages which might lead companies to work together include not only increased turnover, internationalization, evolution of the technology, market access, cost leadership strategy, extending the geographical distribution network but also acquisition of *savoir-faire* and learning. Indeed, the partnership offers opportunities to learn, from the partner, R&D programs or development of activity, information systems, management methods for foreign subsidiaries, etc. In an alliance such as this, a company can feed on its partner's experience. However, there are drawbacks which must be taken into consideration in the context of an alliance. These include cultural differences – seemingly one of the most critical disadvantages. The danger of cultural conflicts may stem from any of four factors: difference in management styles adopted by each of the companies, differences in business culture from one country to another, conflicts due to different long-term objectives and divergence of mentalities, influence and control.

In developing countries, a JV can help local companies to acquire new knowledge from foreign partners in order to fill significant skills gaps.

In the context of this study, we are looking at a JV between two giants in the telecom market, both based in developed countries. Thus, the aim of the move was not to acquire knowledge to reduce an existing shortfall.

Instead, the purpose was to bring together mobile and landline technologies so as to gain a competitive edge. The important this is that the JV can, based on cumulative knowledge from both companies, create new knowledge which offers a long-lasting and renewed competitive advantage.

3.2.1.3. *NSN CCC*

Before presenting the new research area NSN CCC, it would be interesting to present the other party making up the new company NSN CCC with S: the communications company N.

3.2.1.3.1. The company N

Set up in 1865, known for its slogan "Connecting People", and with corporate headquarters in Espoo in Finland, N is active in the telecom domain, and mainly produces mobile phones.

From 1865 to 1967, N was known in the domain of paper, rubber and cables (over the course of around 100 years, N grew into a powerful industry).

From 1968 to 1991, N Corporation occupied a pioneering position in the rapid evolution of mobile communications.

Between 1992 and 1999, in view of the evolution of mobile phone usage, N made that sector its main area of activity. At the turn of the century, N became the world leader in mobile telephony.

Between 2000 and today, N sold its billionth third-generation mobile telephone. The company NSN provides a wireless infrastructure and a hardwired network, communications and service network platforms, as well as offering professional services to operators and service providers.

3.2.1.3.2. NSN

NSN is the appellation given to the company formed by the JV between N and S in the communications domain. This new entity, which includes 600 customers distributed throughout 150 countries all over the world, has its headquarters in Espoo in Finland, just as its parent company, N, does. NSN is already among the three leading world providers of communication services and hopes to take advantage of the growth opportunities represented by the market in terrestrial and wireless communication. This is a market with immense growth prospects, where NSN is already nursing the ambition of becoming the world leader in the provision of communication networks and, by the end of 2015, hopes to connect some 5 billion people across the globe. The Middle East and Africa ("MEA") is the region which ranks highly in the strategy of both NSN's parent companies. The new entity will combine a local presence and *savoir-faire*, strengthened by a global approach and international support. In Tunisia, the success of NSN will depend greatly on its ability to provide high-added-value solutions to its customers, who are essentially telecom operators. The history of S is, to tell the truth, very respectable, given its longstanding presence in Tunisia. For its part, N, which has only recently entered into the region, brings to the table its excellence in the domain of mobile telecom. The merger should facilitate a general synergy, combining N's record in the *networks business* and S's expertise in communication.

The professional activities of NSN CCC are the same as those of SCCC: bid preparation and solution development. However, these activities have been progressively restructured into eight units:

   – the *Consulting* unit provides responses to customers and satisfies their needs with technical solutions composed of products;

   – the *Network Planning and Optimization* unit prepares the design (bid preparation) and optimizes the telecom network (implementation of the project);

   – the *Network Implementation* unit is involved in both processes and is responsible for the realization of the project;

   – the *Applications and Systems Integration* unit provides the customer with integrated technical solutions;

   – the *Security* unit provides technical security solutions to operators;

   – the *Managed Services and Hosting* unit sends professional staff to operators to provide them with highly skilled specialist services;

   – the *Training* unit is the training center not only for customers but also for NSN personnel;

   – the *Care Service* unit takes charge of the maintenance of the products and solutions installed on the customers' premises.

Table 3.1 shows how these units (activities) of SCCC are incorporated into the new NSN structure.

NSN	SCCC
Consulting	TBM – bid management
Network planning and optimization	Project management
Network implementation	Outside plant – engineering
Application and systems integration	TBM – outside plant
Security	RNCC
Managed services and hosting	–
Training	Training
Care service	RNCC

Table 3.1. *Incorporation of the SCCC units into the NSN structure*

Note that only the units (activities) of training and project management are kept entirely as they were in SCCC. The other units (activities) of SCCC are dispersed over several units (activities) in NSN. Finally, the unit (activity) *Managed Services and Hosting* is a new activity of facilities management, and when a researcher last visited NSN, they were unable to tell whether it was based in Tunisia or in another Middle-Eastern country and, which people, if any, from SCCC were involved there.

3.2.2. *Stitching together of operational activities into occupational processes*

Figure 3.1 illustrates the exchanges between SCCC and its environment: sales to its customers, its competitors and the other competence centers run by S. Indeed, when a request from the region of French-speaking Africa or the Middle East is sent to the parent company, the parent company will direct it, through a salesperson, depending on the available skills, to the competence center SCCC in Tunisia, which handle the whole of that region. That salesperson is in direct contact with the end customer and comes into contact with the Bid Management team that will take care of the project. The salesperson communicates the customer's requirements to the Bid Manager in the form of a set of specifications.

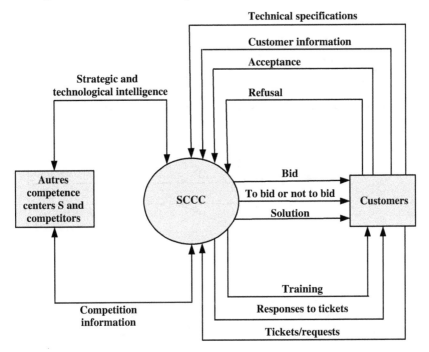

Figure 3.1. *The company's relations with the external environment*

Figure 3.2 shows the exchanges between the two professional processes on which this study focuses (preparation of the customer bid and its implementation) and SCCC's other activities. Indeed, commercial activity, training and technical support are activities which interact with the two business processes in SCCC.

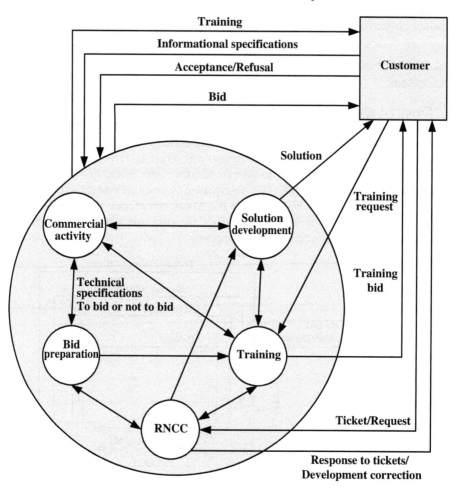

Figure 3.2. *Internal relations between processes and other activities*

A business process corresponds to a set of activities contributing to the achievement of a very definite result, whether that is a tangible good, a service or an informational product. At the heart of the business process is a set of operational activities whereby the product or service destined for the customer is created. In order to be efficient and effective, these activities are based on two other types of activities: support activities, which help to optimize the internal resources of the business process (financial, logistical and human resources) and piloting activities, which are designed to optimize decision-making all along the chain of operational activities. These decisions are either made at an early stage, as part of the strategic piloting, or completely integrated into the operational chain, as part of the operational piloting.

The interweaving of the different departments in the company in terms of business processes (Figure 3.2) takes place when the projects are conducted. This means that teams are working on a project even before the contract is signed – bid preparation (see Figure 3.3) – and after the signing – development of the solution (Figure 3.4): implementation, delivery, installation, training and maintenance.

3.2.2.1. *Project management before the signing of the contract: preparation of the bid*

The *Sales Manager* communicates the customer's requirements to the *Bid Manager* in the form of a set of specifications. The Bid Manager takes charge of constructing the team that works on the project in question, both before and after the signing of the contract, and will monitor the project right through to the end.

In the first stage, there is an initial discussion between the Sales Manager and the Bid Manager. This type of meeting is known as "to bid or not to bid", and at it, the feasibility of the project, as a percentage, is determined. There is a discussion of the general outline of the project, the possibility of offering a product which conforms to the requirements, of taking up an advantageous position in relation to the competition, the definition of a strategy and the importance of the project, etc. Numerous questions are posed by both partners in order to study the probability of winning the project. At the end, they decide either "to bid" or "not to bid".

In the second stage, the Bid Manager appoints the team who is to work on the bid. The team includes permanent members: a *Commercial Bid Manager* and a *Technical Bid Manager*; these are the members who must compulsorily be part of the bid preparation team. Next, on the sales side, we have the *Business Manager*, who sets the customer's general strategy, and the *Commercial Business Manager*, who is in contact with the customer about the commercial side, pricing strategy, etc. From hereon in, we have a team composed of a Bid Manager, a Commercial Bid Manager and a Technical Bid Manager, who form the permanent part of the team. Depending on the needs and the nature of the project, there may also be a person from the *Engineering* department, for reasons of verification, another from the *Project Management* department and member of the *Outside Plant* department. They do not contribute directly to the preparation of the bid, but as the next stage following the bid is the implementation of the project, it is preferable that they should be involved from the very start, so that the partners have as full an understanding as possible, during the next stage, of the difficulties encountered when putting the project into practice. A member of the *Procurement* department might also be invited if it is felt that the equipment requested by the customer includes equipment that is not supplied by the company S, which, therefore, need to be procured elsewhere. There may also be need of a person to handle the difficulties in transporting the equipment from the factories to the customer. We call on *Technical Sales* if the customer requires point-by-point responses and on *Contact Management* in the case of a large project, to facilitate contacts. Thus, it is a team which forms on the fly, depending on the requirements of the bid and the peculiarities of the project.

In the third stage, all the available documents are distributed to the team members and they are invited to a so-called "*kick-off meeting*". At this first important meeting in the bid preparation phase, the chosen strategy and the proposed solution are communicated to everyone involved, and the finer points are discussed because the general outlines have already been discussed at the previous stage, at the meeting between the Sales Manager, the Bid Manager and the Technical Bid Manager. Then, the tasks are distributed and a working schedule is drawn up for each member of the team. This meeting takes place by connection to a single network via a conference telephone. This network – called *net meeting* – allows the members to work in real time on a presentation describing every stage of the project. From that moment on, the bid development may be considered to be under way. Each person works in his/her own area, respecting the set schedule, but there is also a very real group effort within each service, between the services and remotely with members that are geographically far away, given that the members of the team may not necessarily be together on the same site – for example, some of them may be in Germany. This choice depends on the availability of the resources, the type of project, the nature of the technology and the region. There is constant discussion and exchange – face to face at meetings and remotely via the tools *Project View*, *Net meeting*, e-mail, intranet, *Sharenet* (an IMS), telephone, etc. These exchanges relate to critical points which need to be carefully reviewed: situations and difficulties arising where we need others' opinions – for example, on the use of the tool. Communication takes place not only about the content of the project but also about working methods.

Thus, there is a team composed of one person from each department, headed up by the Bid Manager, and subteams in each department under the direction of the department head. Everyone must work in concert toward the same objective: to win the bid.

3.2.2.1.1. The Sales department

The Sales department is the first point of direct contact with the end customer and communicates the customer's demand to the Bid Manager. This is the first contact; so, the Sales department is, to some extent, considered to be the customer interface to which the bid must be addressed.

3.2.2.1.2. The Bid Management department

The Bid Manager handles the bid, coordinates the members of the team, on site and remotely, and manages the contact with the Sales Manager, the Business Manager and the Commercial Business Manager, who are in direct contact with the end customer. The Bid Manager is the main person responsible for the bid preparation. He/she must monitor every stage of the process, from start to finish. The team working on a project is managed by way of internal tasks which take place within the service, such as bringing together everybody's work, imposing a structure on the amassed whole, entering it into the *Project View* tool, establishing the bid within clearly defined directories and checking its final presentation before it is sent to the customer. The team also handles the management of the members' schedules and follow-up in case of any delay, the organization of meetings on the advancement of the project, if it extends for more than three weeks, and the writing of reports. The Bid Manager must be kept informed of any communication between the members, so that he/she is aware of the nature of the difficulties encountered; he/she monitors the situation and helps communication. Thus, s/he needs to ensure he/she has an overall and detailed view of the progress and development of the bid. In order to better perform these tasks, the team uses Project View, which can be used for technical configuration, project management, storage of previous projects and communication via electronic messaging. Following the decision at the initial "to bid or not to bid" meeting, a project session is established (description of the project, list of team members and the arguments behind the decision to "bid"), which must be approved by the hierarchical superiors in Germany. Once approved, work continues on the tool, to which everyone has access. Each member of the team uploads his/her part – technical, commercial or financial – to the Project View session. The role of the Bid Manager is to ensure that everything is running smoothly in the best possible time, which helps to calculate the costs and, therefore, the price to charge the customer. This entire process of bid preparation and project management is done through Project View, which enables everyone involved to communicate and to work together on the project.

3.2.2.1.3. The Technical Bid Management (TBM) department

The TBM defines the solution, justifies the solution chosen and reconfigures the customer's requirements into a list of materials based on a list of equipment, either manually, using the documents, or using a configuration tool. The deliverable expected of the TBM department is the list of materials. The objective of the TBM department in Tunisia is different to that of the one in Germany. In Tunisia, they look for technical expertise, flexibility, communication and quality; in other words, the Tunisian team must communicate well with its partner in Germany and deliver good quality with a great deal of flexibility in order to win the customer's loyalty.

The TBM team has a set of common and complementary skills. Information is circulated within the group so that each member is aware of what the others are doing and the difficulties they are facing. There is a team spirit which forms around a project and another around a technology. Given the enormous quantity of documents, information and time, which is a scarce resource, it is usual to involve a person charged with researching information on a topic and presenting it to the others in a *workshop*, offered to the members of other departments for whom it may be relevant. This service has very close cooperative links with the Bid Management team and a little less so with the other factions.

Figure 3.3 illustrates the above-described process of bid preparation.

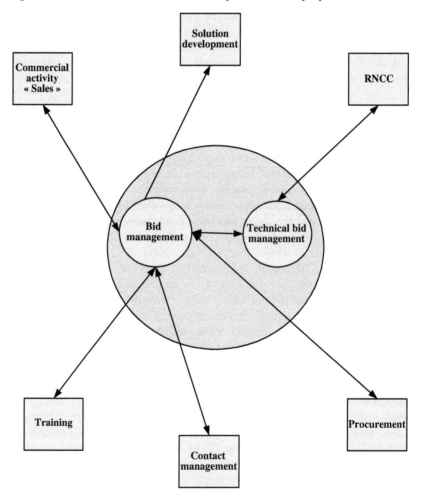

Figure 3.3. *The business process of "bid preparation"*

3.2.2.2. *Project progress (or conduct) after the signing of the contract: solution development*

Once the company has won the bid, the contract is signed and the project is passed to the *Project Management* department, who takes charge of not only constructing a new team but also continues to work with the old team, in a project-continuity logic.

3.2.2.2.1. The Project Management (PM) department

This department takes care of the implementation of the project from the technical and commercial point of view. In the case of a large-scale project, the *Project Manager* collaborates with two new leaders: the *General Project Manager* (GPM) and the *Commercial Project Manager* (CPM). The GPM may be located in Tunisia or in the Middle East and may have certification from the company S or from an international body. Behind the scenes on the project (referred to as *back office*), the PM coordinates all the departments, the factory, the transporters, etc., and constitutes a constant source of support for the GPM and CPM. He/she works with SAP software (Systems, Applications and Products for data processing), including the definition of the project, the members involved in the project, all the sites, a list of materials, orders, delivery, certificate of receipt, all the projected and actual costs, prices, a monthly breakdown of the project's advancement and access to lists of projects in each region and each country. The SAP software is a tool which allows a great deal of transparency of information and a comfortable working method. The *Technical Project Manager* is responsible for the technical part, whilst the CPM takes care of the commercial side of things. The two work in close collaboration and constantly exchange information. In each project, there is a part devoted to training the customer and providing technical support when he/she encounters difficulties. The Project Manager has multiple interfaces and his/her objective is to bring the project to fruition on time, in accordance with the plan, for the lowest possible cost, whilst still aiming to obtain optimum quality and a certain level of performance.

3.2.2.2.2. The Engineering department

The Engineering department works in close collaboration with the PM department on the implementation of the project, in order to deliver a solution to the customer on time; it also works with the implementation service, which is external to SCCC and may be the local company or another company abroad. The Engineering department's role is to analyze the configuration, correct it and rectify it if need be and update that configuration, which dates from the bid preparation stage. It is then helpful to enter into direct contact with the customer or the Sales department to collect or clarify information, rather than going through the Bid Manager, whose role stops once the bid is prepared. The engineering part consists of the configuration of a computer program and the preparation of a database for delivery to the customer, with the aim of integrating a solution into the customer's network. The engineers' true, concrete intervention takes place when the project is being implemented; however, they may also play a part in the bid preparation as a support to the Bid Management and TBM departments. The Engineering department receives, as *input*, all the necessary documents and all the detailed information about the project, from the PM, BM and Sales department, and delivers its *output* in the form of an installation document, startup procedures and the databases to be installed in the telephone exchanges. All these documents are delivered either directly to the customer or via the PM or the realization service.

3.2.2.2.3. The Outside Plant department

This department handles the implementation of the project (installation of communication stations and fiber-optic cables, etc.). It is comparable to the TBM department but for a specific technology, which pertains to external cabling.

3.2.2.2.4. The training institute (TI)

The company SCCC is made up of two entities. The first works directly on behalf of the parent company, whilst the second – the training institute (TI) – functions independently. However, part of that TI is offshore from the point of view of tax and VAT, which is why the TI is on the same site as the SCCC headquarters. Hence, it represents the sole source of profit for the competence center. It also enjoys special prestige because of its training room, its equipment, its showroom, etc. Customers are often impressed by the equipment, the *savoir-faire* and the mobility of the trainers throughout the world. Responsible for the region of Africa and the Middle East, apart from Egypt and South Africa, which have different technologies, this TI works on terrestrial and mobile networks, with mobiles representing 80% of its turnover. This center maintains working relations with S Tunisie, directly with the Tunisian market, directly with the foreign customer or through S Commercial – that is the Sales department for other countries.

Of the 48 training centers run by S worldwide, the center in Tunis is ranked highest and is considered to be the best in the world. Today, its objective is to maintain that position and to improve its current performance in terms of *savoir-faire* in order to survive in the face of competition (from Lebanon, Egypt, etc.). Made up of around 20 people, the team includes trainers, the training line manager (who is not only a trainer but also takes care of one specific technique) and, at the top, the business manager, who takes charge of running and expanding the business and provides support in terms of contracts. The Resource Manager continuously trains the trainers, so that they can achieve a certified level of skill and to ensure they are up-to-date on new developments and the latest technologies. The work of the trainers in itself does not need to be done in a group, except at the very start, when each new trainer is supported by a tutor who has more expertise. At this stage, the work requires a great deal of communication and exchange between the source and the receiver. Once the trainer has reached a particular level of competence, exchange becomes less important than at the start. In addition, given that trainers are often traveling for work, it is difficult to instill a group spirit among the trainers, because of the differing nature and location of their work. In order to remedy this geographical dispersal and create links of exchange and communication, the head of the TI organizes an annual week-long seminar in a hotel in Tunisia, where the whole team comes together.

A workshop was run in August 2006, entitled "Share and update your knowledge". The purpose of this workshop was not solely informational. Over the course of those four days, the trainers trained themselves and one another. In addition, current topics at the time were chosen to form the focus of a debate, during which the participants exchanged their competence and knowledge. The head of the TI felt that this type of get-together should happen twice a year – once for the group as a whole and a second time in subgroups working on the same technologies or who have the same interests. The aim is to encourage the widespread adoption of this type of behavior by the trainers and for it to become their daily norm. In theory, trainers should not have trouble communicating or passing on information. Their problems arise more from individualistic and jealous behaviors: they do not have a problem with communicating their knowledge but want to be seen by others to be – and feel themselves to be – the best. This is a sort of reward or return that they expect. During the workshop, an incentive system was put in place in the form of a reward, ranging from €250 to €1,000 for the best participants. The results of a questionnaire distributed by the Board of Directors show that a large number of the participants are grateful to the organization for running this type of event and for forming teams to work together. These encounters helped achieve the objective of having the event repeated twice a year. This is important because it is an initiative advanced by the trainers themselves, which has not always been the case with other actions established by the board of directors previously (e.g. the method of trainers' self-assessment with a camera, which was not very successful or popular). The objective, according to the head of the TI, is to encourage group work, because the trainers tend to work independently; each one of them has their own skills, but their skills complement one another. Hence, they need to be set common goals and establish shared values in order to see themselves as a group and learn how to consolidate their relationships. Indeed, technically speaking, they perform extremely well. However, this is not sufficient to maintain that performance and evolve. The tool employed by the TI in Tunis and all of S's other TIs is *Training Center*, which supports planning, resource management, charging, invoice certificates management and *e-learning*, which is a new application. In the future, a discussion forum will be integrated, enabling information to be distributed to people who are geographically far away. Thus, it is also possible to create lasting links between the trainers, so that they are not disconnected when they are away for work for long periods of time. Relations with their colleagues in other departments are limited to the context of the bid and the training which comes with it.

3.2.2.2.5. The RNCC

The RNCC offers high-level technical support for the groups of people who maintain, set up and test S equipment and systems. These maintenance groups or Customer Interaction Centers (CICs), work in all countries where S is present, in the form of local support, in direct contact with the customer. Whenever they are faced with the slightest difficulty or a problem with S equipment or systems, customers can contact the CIC in their own country. If the staffs at the CIC are unable to solve the problem, they can, in turn, contact the RNCC in Portugal, linked by satellite to the two subunits in Germany and Tunisia. The RNCC in Tunisia caters for the whole region of French-speaking Africa and France's overseas territories in terms of support, through procedures and intervention on site or remotely. The collaboration of the members of that unit with the other departments of SCCC is very narrow and occasional, except in terms of contributing to advance training on very specific tools. The true collaboration is between Portugal and Germany, via the remote work tool *International case*, which is installed on a server in Austria. All requests from all over the world pass through this server, where they are stored, before being directed in the form of requests transmitted by the call center to Portugal, which redistributes them according to the appropriate regions: either to Tunisia or to Germany. When the request reaches the system in Tunisia, the director or a team member must answer the question within the next 30 minutes, so that the customer receives a response in the best possible time. As there is no knowing where the request comes from or the exact time it was sent, this objective requires careful management to ensure someone is always present in the work room. The work of the team at RNCC Tunisia is to receive requests and attempt to respond to them using the system. If ever they are unable to find a solution, they return to the development stage to attempt to detect the existence of an error. The team has at their disposal a gargantuan database, comprising thousands of tickets and responses each day, as well as development corrections. This database is helpful to use, because if a problem or a fault has been detected in one country, it is certain to be to occur again elsewhere. In view of the diversity of the cases submitted, everyone is trained to be able to carry out all tasks in general, whilst each having a specialization in a few areas (for example, the team leader is expert in mobile technologies, but the rest of the team is not). Thus, every member of the team can begin to lay the foundations of a solution before calling on an expert if needed, meaning that the knowledge held by each of the team members complements that of the others. Integrating and working within this service necessitates a higher-than average level of experience and know-how with S technologies, as a minimum requirement. A new graduate, a person outside of S or an employee with less than 3-year experience cannot directly access a position in this service.

Figure 3.4 illustrates the earlier-mentioned remarks on the process of solution development.

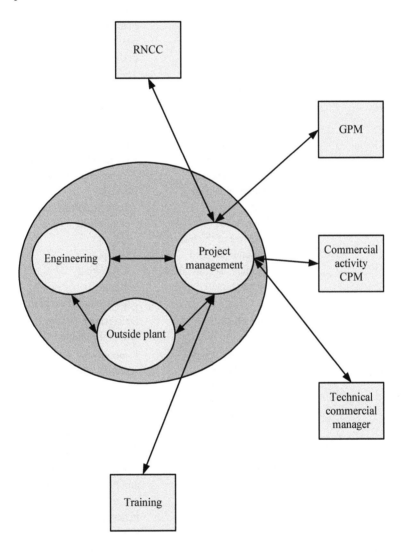

Figure 3.4. *The business process of "solution development"*

The description of each business process in *S Communication Competences Center* (SCCC) is presented in Table 3.2.

	Business process 1: bid preparation	Business process 2: solution development
Objective	To prepare and win a bid.	To implement the project on time, in accordance with the plan, for as low a cost as possible, with good quality and performance.
Input	A set of technical specifications.	The project of the bid after the signing of the contract.
Output	A bid	A solution deliverable to the customer.
Actors	– End customer, – Sales department, – Business Manager, – Commercial Business Manager, – Bid Manager – and the rest of the bid preparation team (Bid Management, Technical Bid Management, etc.)	– Project Management, – General Project Manager, – Commercial Project Manager, – Technical Project Manager, – engineering, – factory, – transporters, – installation, – training – and technical support.
Performance indicator(s)	Winning a bid.	Delivering a quality solution within the allotted time.
Interaction with other processes	– commercial activity, – implementation (continuation of the process after the acceptance of the bid), – etc.	– commercial activity which represents the customer's requirement, – preparation of the bid to ensure it goes forward, – training of the customer in the use of that solution.
Tools used	– Project View, – Intranet, – Sharenet-IMS.	– SAP (Systems, Applications and Products for data processing and ordering of materials), – Intranet, – Sharenet.

Table 3.2. *Descriptions of the business processes in SCCC*

The activities involved in each process are obviously interdependent [THO 67]. This interdependence between the two processes – bid preparation and solution development – is sequential. Indeed, the process of solution development not only begins after the first process has been completed, but it is also conditioned by an outside event: the signing of the contract. Sometimes, in the telecom sector, there may be a significant time gap (2–4 years) between the two processes. However, as soon as the contract is signed, intense reciprocal interdependency arises between those people having participated in the first process and those participating in the second.

3.3. Data collection

The research presented herein is part of an exploratory approach which aims to elucidate the relations which are constructed over the course of time. We are seeking to understand the interactions between actors in their context, which is crucial in order to comprehend them. This accounts for the chosen methodology of the cross-cutting case study with observing participation, enabling the researcher to monitor a process in real time, to take account of the importance of the context and to perform an in-depth analysis of the evolution of the interactions between actors over time.

3.3.1. *Theoretical sampling*

Theoretical sampling can be defined as "the process of data collection to generate theory" ([YIN 89] cited in Hlady Rispal [HLA 02, p. 68]). In the context of qualitative research, sampling aims to obtain a theoretical representation, rather than a statistical one: immediate or more progressive in the case of rooted theory [MIL 94]. These authors indicate that samples may evolve during the course of the research (certain actors can recommend other samples). Hence, it is important to delimit the scope of the study (in the case at hand, the focus is on two occupational processes: the team working on the bid preparation and the team working on solution development), and create a structure which helps to uncover and explain the fundamental processes of the study. Miles and Huberman [MIL 94] recommend looking at the following sampling parameters: media, actors, events and processes. However, as noted by Charreire-Petit [CHA 95], in research aimed at understanding a process, the last parameter cannot be used, because it is, in itself, the object of analysis.

For this research, we wish to find cases which help to understand and explain the conditions which favor KM within a working group. In line with the literature review and with the conceptual framework used, we shall try to select a case corresponding to the following criteria:

– *Medium*: a multicultural environment, because the competence center where the study is based belongs to the parent company situated in Germany and then Finland, following the NSN merger. It is located, geographically speaking, in Tunisia, for material and financial advantages and reasons of proximity, and responds to a demand from the MEA region. In addition, this explains the choice of the communication sector (terrestrial and mobile telephony) in which the professional occupations are unstable and the teams are faced with uncertainty and the mobility of their missions;

– *Actors*: possibility of observing and conducting interviews with different actors in the field. More specifically, the sample pertains to the two most important business processes in the life of the center (bid preparation and solution development), around which project teams are constructed and come together, with their members belonging to different departments;

–*Events*: possibility of observing or participating in different events and projects at the competence center (formal meetings and informal interactions, in particular). The researcher was present in the field just at the moment of a major event in the company's history: the merger of the two companies S and N. Hence, she was able to observe the atmosphere before, during and after the merger.

In the context of this research, the population representative of the sample evolved over the course of the three phases of the study, characterized by three contexts: SCCC, NSN CCC in a period of a merger and restructuring and NSN CCC in a period of stability (18 months after the merger):

– *During the exploratory phase*, the President and CEO, the heads of the different departments of SCCC, a project manager and an engineer were interviewed.

– *During the intensive phase*, the sample is mainly based on the project team working on the two main business processes in the competence center (bid preparation and solution development) and involving all the departments without exception (*Bid Management, Technical Bid Management, Project Management, Engineering, Outside Plant*, Training Institute, RNCC and *Procurement*). The 35 people interviewed (22 men and 13 women) have various backgrounds (engineers, technicians or sales engineers) and belong to the seven departments mentioned earlier, aged between 23 and 40 years, with some being highly experienced and some novices, all of Tunisian nationality (with or without experience abroad). All of them are employees of SCCC (only one person out of those interviewed has worked for N in the past). This sample was selected from among various forms of grouping of individuals in the field of the research:

- project teams, which are built around the business processes of bid preparation and solution development for the customer: a group of local people situated both within and between services, working locally and remotely with colleagues from the parent company or other centers in the region throughout the life of a project before and after the signing of the contract,

- workshops, which are constructed around a theme or a center of interest and constitute a support for the project team,

- initiatives of groups of people similar to communities of practice, founded by certain people wishing to broadcast and share their expertise,

- the group of trainers at twice-yearly seminars for a dynamic exchange of competences,

- the set day: a meeting is organized for one set day each month, in most of the departments. This enables the heads of department to take stock with their teams, from the point of view of work, projects and state of advancement.

During this phase, the main technologies and tools on which the study focused were: the company intranet and Sharenet – IMS.

– *During the checking phase*, it was deemed necessary to return to the scene 18 months after the merger of S and N and the creation of the new company, NSN. During this phase, multiple formal and informal interviews were conducted with the new human resources director, who plays a very important role in the life of the new company. An attempt was made to re-interview the same people as in the sample from the intensive phase, but in view of the fact that certain people had left, the increased mobility characteristic of the new structure and the constraints on some people, in actual fact only 15 people could be interviewed. Thus, the characteristics of this sample are the same as that from the intensive phase.

3.3.2. *Data collection*

The approach adopted here to gather the data is essentially inspired by the recommendations given by Glaser and Strauss [GLA 67] and Eisenhardt [EIS 89a]. A concerted effort was made to have a very open approach to the collection of data so as to promote the emergence of new elements, not directly linked to definite frameworks from existing theories [GLA 67]. Thus, the initial interviews were very open, as was the collection of secondary data.

3.3.2.1. *Type of data collected*

The research yielded three types of data.

3.3.2.1.1. Interviews with the actors

Semi-directive interviews were conducted in accordance with an interview guide, recorded and transcribed. Informal interviews were also conducted but not recorded.

3.3.2.1.2. Documents

The researcher had at their disposal a number of documents in the form of internal notes, reports on meetings, technical specifications, models, reports, examples of bids, PowerPoint presentations, organigrams, screengrabs and the results of the self-evaluation questionnaires.

3.3.2.1.3. Observations

The observations are either non-participant or participant (on teamwork situations, informal convivial occasions, exchanges between actors, etc.) and transcribed in the research journal in the form of notes with digital photographs. The researcher actively participated in real KM situations in the company: organization and support of networks such as communities of practice and working groups, in a workshop entitled "KM", reporting on the existing technological tools, organization of inter-departmental or inter-functional meetings with the support of the management, attending the trainers' workshops and seminars, English lessons and certain training sessions as well.

These data were collected throughout the three phases of the study and served as the basis for data triangulation [JIC 79].

3.3.2.2. *The different stages of data collection*

During the 36 months (July 2006 to August 2009) devoted to the study of the field, the research alternated between various formulas of study, ranging from external observation (I) to active participation (II):

– I: observation and interviews at two different times: from August to September 2006 (*exploratory phase*) and from July to August 2009 (*verification phase*);

– II: otal immersion over 12 months with active participation from January to December 2007 (*intensive phase*).

3.3.2.2.1. Entry into the field

In April 2006, the proposal for a research project was sent to the company. During May 2006, an e-mail exchange was established with the President and CEO of SCCC, who was interested in the idea of the study. In July 2006, at an initial informal interview, the context of the research, the focal issue and the objectives was presented to the President and CEO of SCCC in Tunisia. Then, they discussed the possibilities of access to the daily goings-on in the company. Having agreed, the President and CEO of SCCC put us in contact with the person coordinating the project – the head of the TBM department, who was also informally in charge of the tasks of communication and information sharing within the company. From that point on, the study was conducted in three phases.

The exploratory phase (August to September 2006)

During this initial period, we familiarized ourselves with the company (the place and the people), met actors in the field who were very different in terms of their role and their position in the center (directors, project managers, engineers, etc.), and very openly garnered information about the company (its domain of activity, the occupations it holds, organigrams, etc.), its knowledge and know-how perimeter and its KM tools (IMS, Sharenet, Intranet, etc.). Finally, we sought to define the population who were of interest for the research at hand and from the point of view of the issue being examined in the next phase. Ten semi-directive interviews were conducted, numerous informal contacts forged and data of all kinds collected (the organigram from July 2006, screenshots from the intranet, results of an internal questionnaire and a few contacts in the form of business cards). Once the study's preliminary results had been presented to the President and CEO of SCCC, he gave his consent for it to continue to the next stage. The intervening period between these two phases in the study – September 2006 to January 2007 – was characterized by the concretization and consolidation of the principles of the NSN merger. The period of the next phase constitutes a new chapter in the company's existence.

A phase of intensive study (January 2007 to December 2007)

Our presence in the field during this phase can be qualified as total immersion. After the introductory period, we envisaged to continue the study in a variety of ways. Over the course of 12 months, we involved ourselves fully on site, participating in the activities of the different departments and assisting the people in charge of projects. This participation helped when analyzing the situations encountered in the field, identifying points where serious focus was needed and formulating proposed solutions appropriate for the context. Thus, we:

– attended team meetings with the project teams in charge of preparing a bid or developing a solution, both within departments and between different ones;

– attended workshops and informal opportunities for exchanges;

– attended one of the seminars organized by the training center for exchange and dynamics of competences;

– attended training sessions, English classes, etc.;

– participated in the organization and support of networks such as communities of practices and working groups, analysis of technical tools with the help of the IT department, organization of inter-departmental or inter-functional meetings in accordance with the management;

– attempted to make an evaluative assessment of the company's KM activities (before, during and after the merger).

In parallel to these activities, we conducted 35 interviews with the relevant population, with the aim of analyzing and studying the conditions of development of KM between the members of the project team and the practices of use of collaborative and KM tools.

Verification phase (July to August 2009)

Back in the field for this stage of the study, we refined certain hypotheses, tested conflicting explanations and explored additional avenues. During this period, we conducted 15 formal interviews and multiple informal interviews and discussions. In addition, many further documents and demonstrations were collected, pertaining to the main evolutions of the KM and communications management tools, in the form of screengrabs.

Table 3.3 gives an overview of data collection activities.

	Phase 1 *August to September 2006*	**Phase 2** *January to December 2007*	**Phase 3** *July to August 2009*
Field	SCCC	Merger with N	NSN
Phase of research	Exploratory study	Intensive study Total immersion	Verification phase Regular return to the field
Data collection	10 interviews	35 interviews	15 interviews
Researcher's status	Observation	Observation and participant observation	Observation

Table 3.3. *Data collection (overview)*

Ultimately, data were regularly collected in the field over the course of nearly 3 years (6 months before the merger, a year whilst the merger was taking place, and 18 months after it). This meant we were able to observe the process almost in real time, over an extended period. In total, we conducted 60 semi-directive interviews and attended a great many formal and informal meetings. To support the data collection, a semi-directive interview guide was used (several versions were used during the different stages of the study). Those data are supplemented by the notes in the research journal and by the corpus of documents collected.

3.3.2.3. *Interviews and observations*

The semi-directive interview guide focuses on a few major themes. The interlocutors were allowed to touch on those themes freely, and effort was made to allow them to elaborate on potentially interesting points [DEM 03]. The semi-directive interview guide was greatly modified and endowed with detail after the exploratory phase, in order to take account of the initial lessons drawn from the study. For each interview, we took notes and recorded the discussion. The interlocutors showed no objection to the use of the Dictaphone. Each time, we explained the objectives of the study and told them that the recording could be stopped at any time. Participants were also offered a copy of the transcription of their interviews. The 60 interviews conducted lasted between 30 minutes and 2 hours. The notes, written up within a few hours of each interview, helped supplement the recordings on certain points, and this initial transcription also enriched the investigations under way, without having to wait for a complete transcription of the recordings (this task is much more time-consuming and was done afterward).

During the intensive phase of the study, we spent an average of 4 days a week on site, over the course of 12 months. This presence was facilitated by the fact of having a work station on site and participating in a number of tasks in the company's activities.

As per Mucchielli's [MUC 96] recommendations, our observations and comments were systematically transcribed in a research journal. This journal enabled us to systematically record contextual factors, observations made on the fly such as the ambiance at the meetings, in the workshops, during training sessions or in the working teams, in the corridors and during the coffee break, at lunchtime or, indeed, walking to the carpark; all this information, collected informally, is deemed to be useful in refining our understanding of the processes and the context.

3.3.2.4. *Secondary data*

In parallel, throughout the whole length of the study, various documents were collected, which allow us to deepen our analysis (minutes of meetings, technical specifications, documents, screengrabs, etc.). In summary, the interviews of the different actors in the company constitute the primary data – and the main data – for this research. The internal and external documents represent the secondary data needing to be analyzed. In addition to this, our total immersion in the field was of vital importance. Indeed, generally speaking, and specifically in the context of qualitative research, we have stressed the advantage to, and importance of, total immersion of a researcher in the field. In the view of Avenier [AVE 89], a researcher must place him/herself as a neutral observer of the phenomenon and must be careful not to interfere with it.

The use of these three modes of data collection (interviews, observations noted in a research journal, documents and secondary data) serves as the basis for data triangulation [JIC 79, DEN 94].

3.4. Processing of the collected data

The purpose of data processing is to specify the approach adopted to analyze the collected data. This approach was carried out in two successive stages: analysis of the thematic content of the interviews, followed by multi-angular analysis of all the documents collected. Before going into the phase of analysis of the gathered data, we shall first present the approach adopted.

3.4.1. *Thematic content analysis*

For the analysis and interpretation of the data collected during this exploratory study, the content analysis method [BER 52, BAR 77] was chosen. This method is based on an analysis of thematic content using matrices inspired by the checklist matrix developed by Miles and Huberman [MIL 91].

The objective here is to derive a set of explanations as to the conditions favoring and/or hampering KM within a group. In order to construct such explanations and discover the conditions that facilitate the development of the knowledge resource, the study was based on the literature, our observations and understanding of the behaviors in terms of KM in the field.

For this study, thematic content analysis was chosen because this technique is in line with the objective of the research, which is to interpret the actors' individual perceptions and their behavior toward the collection, sharing and creating of useful knowledge among them.

The first stage of the analysis of the content of the transcribed interviews consisted of an analysis, interview by interview. Then, the second stage was a thematic analysis of all of the interviews. The sequential analyses of each interview enabled the researcher to identify all of the themes dealt with by the interviewees, and the thematic analysis of all the interviews conducted led to the compilation of a precise thematic dictionary.

In addition, qualitative data analysis (of which the best-known technique is content analysis) is the most widely used method to study interviews or qualitative observations [KRI 03]. This method involves transcribing the qualitative data, constructing an analysis grid, codifying the information collected and processing it. The analysis describes the material from the inquiry and looks at its meaning. This section goes into detail about the main stages of content analysis [AND 05].

Content analysis is based on the construction of a referential framework against which to compare the content of the text. Depending on the objectives of the study, this framework may be established in advance or progressively be constructed over the course of the analysis of the collected information. The content analysis may be lexical or thematic: a lexical analysis draws on the redundancy of language to examine the terms that are most frequently employed. A thematic analysis is based on the analysis of the meanings of the respondent's discourse. As a result, each response in an interview or fragment of discourse is assigned to one of the thematic categories which the examination has revealed.

3.4.1.1. *Transcription of the interviews*

Before beginning the analysis, the first stage is to take an inventory of the information collected and record that information in written form [AND 05]. This text, known as a *verbatim*, represents the raw data from the investigation. Indeed, the transcription organizes the material from the inquiry in a format that is directly accessible by analysis.

3.4.1.1.1. Nature of the qualitative data collected

The qualitative data collected, which are in the form of texts (words, phrases and linguistic expression) and symbolic information (gestures, tone of voice, impressions, etc.), arise from the transcription of the interviews, notes from observations on the ground, various types of written documents (reports, minutes, articles and publications on the intranet) and previously published texts (press articles, reviews, etc.). To serve the objective of the study at hand, once they are analyzed, those data are used to document, describe and evaluate a situation or a phenomenon, to compare and explain the conditions for development of the knowledge resource within a group.

3.4.1.1.2. Transcription of the interviews

This task is done by hand [SIL 00]. It involves the word-for-word noting of everything that the respondent says, without altering the text at all, without interpretation and without abridgment. Transcription is a lengthy and thankless task. Andreani and Conchon [AND 05] estimate that, for each hour of interview time, it takes 2 to 3 hours to type the 6–8,000 words into the text processing program Word. In this case, the task took much longer, given the fact that there were words said in other languages (Arabic, English and German) which needed to be translated into French.

3.4.1.1.3. Observation notes

These notes are edited and transcribed. Their purpose is to reveal what we observed. They contain everything which needs to be said – even the smallest details. They enable us to take account of certain details that reveal useful ideas. The observation notes give an account of the habits linked to the communication and interaction between the members of the organization. They show the rules followed, the habits, the difficulties encountered, the adjustment practices and the deviations that they entail.

3.4.1.2. *Codification of the data and analysis of their thematic content*

Codification explores, line by line and stage by stage, the texts of every interview and all the observations formulated [BER 03]: "It describes, classifies and transforms raw qualitative data on the basis of the analysis grid. It is a lengthy and painstaking process, which is done manually, and for which no automated system exists" [AND 05].

The qualitative data having been transcribed, an analysis grid is constructed before going on to codify them. This framework is made up of criteria and indicators, which are called the analytical categories. That analysis grid, also known as a "thematic dictionary", is the foundation upon which the analysis of the interviews is based. In view of the total corpus collected after the complete transcription of all 60 interviews constituting the base of the content analysis, the thematic dictionary was constructed in two stages.

First of all, an initial analysis grid was constructed, including the themes and subthemes predefined in the literature. A first level of analysis by comparison between the collected corpus and the provisional thematic dictionary revealed elements that seemed pertinent which had not been sufficiently dealt with by the prior literature and, thus, by the initial analysis grid.

Second, the original conceptual framework was enriched and, thus, a definitive analysis grid constructed, taking account of the elements defined in the literature and those that had emerged from the research field. The grid used for the codification of the transcribed interviews is made up of categories defined by themes and subthemes, which have a definition fed by the literature and refined by descriptors or codes.

The approach adopted drew inspiration from the typological analysis by Miles and Huberman [MIL 94]. To begin with, a number of fairly general themes were identified and defined, on the basis of the pre-existing literature, the conceptual framework and the research questions. Then, a list of codes was drawn up and reviewed many times, as the data collection and analysis progressed and the literature was consulted again. Next, certain elements were grouped together into broader categories using a thematic codification as discussed by Miles and Huberman [MIL 94], where sometimes new themes emerge.

All of the formal interviews which were recorded and transcribed in their entirety have been codified. However, it has not been possible to codify the research journal and the collected documents, as they are mainly used as the counterpoint to the analyses, to enrich them and enhance their accuracy.

The initial (general) thematic dictionary includes categories, themes, subthemes and codes. This thematic dictionary has been simplified since our time in the field and in light of the literature review and research model put forward, giving rise to the analysis grid. On the basis of that grid, we matched verbatim extracts to each code. The analysis grid matches the components and constructs of the conceptual research model against those of the thematic dictionary. This grid will be enriched throughout the coding process with themes and subthemes emerging both from new literature and the content of the interviews – that is from the field during the three phases of the study.

3.4.2. Multi-angular analysis

Despite how rich the content-analysis method is, it is still useful to perform a multi-angular analysis of all the data gathered, after having analyzed the topical content. This multi-faceted analysis was based on the results of the topical content analysis performed previously and on the research journal and secondary data. The purpose was for these two types of data to confirm or qualify the results of the interview study. These data were analyzed in their own right, though in less depth than the study of the interviews conducted during the research.

The research journal includes notes, impressions and reactions from our observations (participating or otherwise) during our intensive presence in the field (12 months) – for example during regular participation in meetings and training sessions. It represents a catalog of all the notes taken when observing the actors at work, in the training sessions, around the coffee machine, engaged in informal discussions or at events organized by the staff, such as leaving parties for certain colleagues, etc. Other documents gathered from the intranet or from colleagues tend to be non-confidential documents which offered a fuller understanding of the company's areas of activity, the content of a bid or a project, the working principle of a project team or the content of working tools (principles of use, functions, etc.).

Note that with qualitative research, the academic validity and reliability of the results must be demonstrated by a frank report on the method of data collection and processing. According to Thiétart *et al.* [THI 96], "Reliability is assessed, firstly, on the basis of comparison of the results found by the different researchers when there are several, and secondly, on the basis of the codification of the raw data gleaned from the interviews, documents or observations" (p. 269). There are specific methodological criteria that are used to evaluate the academic validity and reliability of a piece of research. Indeed, with a view to generalizing the results, it is important to ensure they are credible, transferable and reliable:

– *Credibility* is based on the triangulation of the data and data sources. In the context of this research, the data collection resulted in the triangulation of those data:

- participant observation and non-participant observation: our intensive presence on the ground over the course of 12 months involved participation in the active, daily life of the company and observation of the actors and the various interactions in their workspace. The observations were recorded in a research journal,

- centered semi-directive interviews: 60 formal interviews, recorded and transcribed during the three phases of the study (15 during the first phase, 35 during the intensive phase and 15 during the third phase),

- internal and external documents: such documents were collected during all three phases of the study – primarily documents taken from the company intranet, documents explaining the usage principle behind working tools, etc.,

- varied data sources, putting questions to actors in different professional area (bid–project), with different profiles (commercial–technical) and different hierarchical levels (director–team member);

– *Transferability* pertains to whether the developed theory can be applied to a similar situation in a similar context or whether, as Miles and Huberman [MIL 03] put it: "the study's conclusions have broader significance". With this research, we set out to convey the context of the particular case study as accurately as possible, by way of a description of the general framework of the organization under study and its main features and to clearly describe the methodological approach adopted.

– The *reliability* of the results obtained has already been proven by the methodology, by long-term involvement in the field, triangulation of the garnered data and contextualization of the case study. Our intensive presence in the field is highly effective, in that it helps to detect any contradictions between the explanations advanced by us and by those given by the interviewees. A second external researcher, who is skilled in the domain of qualitative research and well informed about the study, also contributed to the content analysis. The purpose of this intervention was to test the interpretation of the data made by us, the primary researcher, by verifying the pertinence and consistency of the data codification by a double codification process.

As regards the internal and external validity of the case study, account was taken of the aforementioned methodological criteria to neutralize the criticisms often leveled at the single case study in terms of its validity beyond that single context, in accordance with the recommendations of Yin [YIN 94]. Note that, in the singular case study, the use of theory helps improve the external validity, in the view of Yin [YIN 03a].

4

Case Study

This chapter presents the results of the research in the field, in light of our model of the "learning organization design". The division of the chapter reflects the three phases of the cross-cutting study:

– the first phase: the company S, before its merger (section 4.1);

– the second phase: the period of the merger between the two companies S and N (section 4.2);

– the final phase: the new company NSN, after the merger (section 4.3).

For each of these three phases, the analysis of the results will be presented in accordance with the logic of the components of the learning organization model: the strategy, the incentive systems, the people, the knowledge management system (KMS) technology and the structure.

4.1. Design of the learning organization SCCC (before the merger)

During this phase, the objective was to collect data that would elucidate the company's strategy, its structure and the different professional roles involved, whilst attempting to identify the role played by knowledge management (KM) in the company's strategy. Thus, we identified the population targeted in the company and furthered her knowledge of the different professional activities to which the company's KM applies.

4.1.1. *Strategy*

4.1.1.1. *KM: a strategic objective*

KM was part of the strategy employed by S Communication Competences Center Tunisia (SCCC), and this manifested itself in different ways – particularly in the importance attached to, and diversity of, the training offered. The presence of the S training center constituted a significant support for on-site training – particularly because of the constant presence of a consultant in the company.

Various integration devices were used, with a view to encouraging knowledge exchange:

– workshops for information and integration of new members, organized in the context of soirées in prestigious hotels;

– "Welcome to the new member" dinners enabled colleagues to get to know new members of the organization and facilitated their integration into the group. This was an initiative implemented by higher management when the SCCC was set up. It also demonstrated that the company's strategy was favorable to socialization, integration and communication between the teams;

– the existence of open working spaces and of the coffee room encouraged communication, socialization and essentially all types of informal exchange of tacit knowledge.

The establishment of a KMS, intended mainly for the project teams, also appeared to indicate the strategic nature of KM. Thus, different approaches and initiatives demonstrated the important place held by KM in the company's overall strategy.

4.1.1.2. *Support of the managers for KM*

Significant differences can be observed from one department to another. There was divergence between the company's overall strategy and the strategies of the department heads as regard KM and the adoption of KM tools. Indeed, the discourse from SCCC management was favorable to KM, but the department heads were offered no incentive to use it. The support of the managers for KM techniques and for the adoption of the associated tools – which the literature tells us is of prime importance – was very random between the different departments. It depended on the mentality of the department head, his/her experience in that area and his/her ability to manage a team.

Sometimes, the atmosphere within the teams was not very favorable to knowledge sharing – notably because of the diversity of the team members (in terms of their age, nationality, training, social status, experience, language, character and culture), but especially because the hierarchical superior did nothing to create synergy and encourage the team members to cooperate in this manner. In this case, the hierarchical superior's intervention was limited to the operational level, to giving orders and collecting results; he/she had no communication- and team-management abilities to create a better atmosphere and favorable group ambiance and ensure that this diversity was an asset for the team and the company. In certain cases, also, the hierarchical superiors systematically refused to provide the members of their team with training. Some such hierarchical superiors never organized meetings to stay abreast of the problems that the members of their teams might be experiencing, or "set days", or even feedback meetings so the team members could improve their work in the future and correct their mistakes. This neglect on the part of the management was highly demotivating in certain departments. The lack of supervision, feedback (whether positive or negative) or experience feedback from the hierarchical hierarchical superiors regarding the work done by the team members created a demotivation. Indeed, for an individual, lack of confidence in his/her own knowledge and skills and lack of feedback from his/her hierarchical superior can demotivate him/her and inhibit individual learning. This often results in increased passivity and a reduction in contribution to the work of the team and in transfer of knowledge to the other members.

On the other hand, the presence of a group leader with a multicultural outlook and the ability to make that heterogeneity an asset for the team facilitates the convergence and homogenization of the viewpoints of the team members.

IN SUMMARY.– The development of KM was among the strategic objectives, as clearly stated by the head of SCCC Tunisia. However, these favorable potentials were not universally implemented by the department heads, and there was limited use of the associated tools.

4.1.2. *Incentive systems*

4.1.2.1. *The financial incentive system*

By comparison with other companies in the same sector, SCCC's human resources policy was felt not to be very active, in terms both of salaries and career development. Thus, the financial incentive system was poor. In addition, the disparity of salaries between local personnel and expatriate personnel was perceived as being highly unfair and was often the subject of informal discussions. However, this salary gap did not create a problem between Tunisian and foreign workers. Their working relationships were good, based on cooperation and trust. Instead, the staff demonstrated a lack of trust in the management.

Other tangible perks were available, such as mobile phones and phone plans, trips and missions abroad. These were awarded at will by the team leaders.

The financial incentive system and tangible perks had no effect on the behavior of the team members in terms of learning and sharing. The motivation to help others was based more on relational aspects, team spirit and the company's values than on financial incentives.

4.1.2.2. *The non-financial incentive system*

4.1.2.2.1. Training

The training was deemed to be of very good quality, with excellent continuity and sufficient richness. It was composed of a wide range of devices, some of which were specifically for the project teams – the target population for the KMS:

– operational and technical training: training on the job, training with new techniques, new products, etc.;

– personal development: training for constructive communication, time management, *Task Force, Game Factory*;

– language training: English, German, etc.;

– training within the company, at external organizations and abroad at Bath Academy in England;

– the annual workshop for the trainers, the main aim of which was the exchange of experiences. Indeed, trainers were often traveling for work in other countries, rarely came into contact with one another and were almost never all present in the same place at the same time. Hence, this workshop represented an opportunity to bring almost all of them together, once a year. However, this judicious initiative was deemed to be insufficient; so, the former CEO of SCCC had arranged for it to be a biannual event;

– the "set day": many department heads felt it was helpful to organize a meeting, once a month, with their teams in order to stay abreast of the progress of the work, the projects and the training requirements.

All these initiatives had an impact not only on the activities of knowledge acquisition and collection but also on the activities of sharing, transfer and creation of new knowledge.

As everybody said, "S is an excellent training school", and the possibilities were multiple, as demonstrated earlier. This is particularly important in the rapidly changing world of telecommunications, where training is necessary and very costly.

Perceived within SCCC as a genuine advantage, the offer of training constituted a sustained incentive.

4.1.2.2.2. Organizational culture

The organizational culture was favorable for KM, because it encouraged exchange and formal (and especially, informal) learning. The culture of SCCC was known for its excellent policy on the training and integration of new arrivals.

4.1.2.2.3. Trust

Trust in the management: There was a lack of trust in the direct hierarchical superior and the management in general. This was due to past promises not having been kept and lack of recognition of the commitment of the project teams to their work. The following facts illustrate our point:

– Promises were rarely kept by the management, in terms of bonuses, salary increases and career progression.

– The team members were considered to be subordinates, with no direct access to the customers. Direct relations with the customers were monopolized by the hierarchical superior, who played the *front-office* role, leaving his/her team to perform the *back-office* functions.

– There was a lack of communication and dialog between certain hierarchical superiors and their teams. In certain cases, the new arrivals had difficulty integrating. In other cases, the hierarchical superiors did not provide their teams with the necessary training;

– Frequently, there was a lack of contextual framing and feedback by the hierarchical superior.

– Certain department heads were hostile to the use of the KMS.

Trust between colleagues: In response to the shortcomings of the direct management, there was a great deal of solidarity among the collaborators in our target population. The members of the teams exchanged with one another a great deal and shared their knowledge. This phenomenon constituted an opportunity to develop each person's skills and to create new knowledge on the basis of exchanges between groups. When the department heads did not pass on information about the KMS, the collaborators in question learned to use it from their colleagues.

The disparity of financial conditions between locals and expatriates had no impact on the relations between the colleagues. Thus, during "training on the job", knowledge transfer from the Germans to the new Tunisian recruits went well. Although they had expressed their anger and lack of trust in the management, the Germans never hesitated, first, to transfer their knowledge and know-how to the Tunisians and, second, to create links of friendship and cooperation between colleagues.

IN SUMMARY.– The financial incentive system did not constitute a major reference within SCCC. The non-financial incentives – not only training but also organizational culture and trust among colleagues – encouraged KM. The lack of trust in the management did not appear to hamper the KM process.

4.1.3. *People*

4.1.3.1. *Individual characteristics*

Generally speaking, individual characteristics such as age and gender did not seem to have any impact on the individuals' behavior in terms of KM and the use of the associated tools.

4.1.3.2. *Language*

In certain cases, the mastery of the German language helped facilitate the integration of the Tunisians who spoke it.

However, sometimes, the German language constituted an obstacle to communication and to integration – for example when the hierarchical superiors only spoke German and had no command of French, Arabic or English, which was, nevertheless, the official language used in SCCC. In this case, the hierarchical superiors made no effort whatsoever, preferring to communicate only with one another. This type of behavior caused a split in certain teams, giving rise to two clans. A dominant clan, made up of the expatriates and the hierarchical superior, received and discussed the bids. The dominated clan, made up primarily of Tunisian nationals, simply received work instructions to carry out. This resulted in a lack of integration and involvement, the demotivation of the personnel and a lack of trust in the hierarchical superiors.

4.1.3.3. *National culture*

At this point, two national cultures (German and Tunisian) coexisted, but those cultural differences had no impact on the KM. The behaviors of knowledge sharing or non-sharing and use or non-use of the tools were noted equally in people of different national cultures.

The behavior which, favorably or unfavorably, influenced the KM was primarily due to a question of conviction, experience and integration in the team rather than to a question of national culture.

In addition, the national culture of SCCC's customers is taken into account by the teams and is appropriated throughout the length of the project.

IN SUMMARY.– The individual characteristics and national culture of the teams did not seem to have any effect on KM. The lack of language skills/the linguistic barrier between the hierarchical levels has a negative effect on KM.

4.1.4. *Technology: KMS*

4.1.4.1. *The functions of KMSs*

KM tools are made up of the following elements.

4.1.4.1.1. S Worldwide intranet

The company's global intranet is widely used from all over the world for electronic messaging, finding information, documents and useful contacts. This intranet enables the project teams to access other tools (Sharenet-IMS).

4.1.4.1.2. S Tunisia intranet

The intranet run by S Tunisia is less rich in content and functions and exhibits many problems and technical limitations.

4.1.4.1.3. Sharenet-IMS

Sharenet-IMS is a tool owned and used by SCCC, installed in 1997–1998: a KMS which is both interactive and integrative, to use the terms employed by Alavi and Leidner [ALA 01]. It comprises two interfaces:

– *The Sharenet interface*, which is an exchange tool in the form of a discussion forum. It is judged to be interactive and effective, because of the quality of its answers, which is recognized by its users. It helps to construct a list of contacts whilst identifying experts in different useful and interesting domains. This tool, which may be considered a tool for the creation and use of knowledge based on social processes and inter-individual interactions, places emphasis on the issue of exchange.

– *The Information Management Systems* (*IMS*) *interface*: This interface offers access to a database – known as the project library in SCCC – containing technical and commercial documentation about the products and the project solutions. This tool provides two functions: first, it manages the information history relating to the projects, and second, it offers the facility to search for documents and projects and to identify useful people to contact. On a technical level, this tool allows the information to be updated quickly and offers access to that information in sufficient conditions of security (access protected by a login and password).

4.1.4.2. *The characteristics of use of KMSs*

Two characteristics of use of KMSs are dominant in SCCC: the lack of generalization of these tools and their optional use in the context of the implementation of the business processes: bid preparation and solution development.

Of the people contributing to these professional processes, we can distinguish three categories of KMS users: daily users, occasional users and non-users.

Five cases of *daily users* have been identified:

– case 1: the experienced user, who usually has previous experience in Munich;

– case 2: the user informed and assisted in the use of the tool by a department head who is different to his/her own immediate hierarchical superior;

– case 3: the user who, following a career move, must use the tool in his/her new activities;

– case 4: the user informed and trained by colleagues, whose initial training has little to do with the telecom sector;

– case 5: the user having accidentally discovered the tool on the company intranet.

Similarly, five cases of *occasional users* were identified:

– case 1: the indirect user; a colleague uses the tool to access and procure for him/her all the information needed for his/her work;

– case 2: the occasional user who is unsatisfied, because he/she is conscious of the tool's inadequate performances in comparison to those of the parent company in Munich which he/she has used previously;

– case 3: the occasional user who has an insufficient command of all the tool's functions;

– case 4: the occasional user whose activities do not require daily use of the tool;

– case 5: the occasional user having limited access to the tool (not authorized to use all its functions).

Among the *non-users*, three types of profiles were identified:

– profile 1: people who are not authorized to use the tool;

– profile 2: people who prefer face-to-face contact and people who do not see the advantage of the tool;

– profile 3: those who are unaware of the tool's existence.

4.1.4.3. *Ease of use, perceived usefulness and perceived results of the KMS*

Overall, the KMSs were not considered to be easy to use: they had a slow response time, there was no standardization of the data and these tools were not integrated. The perceived usefulness and results of the KMSs were highly random because of the usage characteristics.

IN SUMMARY.– The use of the KMS was random and generally low. Its perceived usefulness was deemed to be less than that of the tools available to the parent company in Germany and the other countries where the group operates.

4.1.5. *Structure*

4.1.5.1. *Hierarchical levels*

The Tunisian unit had 202 employees, but it represented a very small set within a large, and very hierarchical, group. Deemed to be too pyramidal, the structure within which SCCC evolved made it difficult for the project teams to have contact with the directors and customers. This type of structure does not facilitate the implementation of a KM approach in the company. The lack of fluidity in the contact between directors and employees may even constitute a terrain unfavorable to KM.

4.1.5.2. *Business processes*

The business process-based structure improves coordination, the establishment of common goals and shared interests. This reciprocal interdependence of the activities, both intra-processes and inter-processes, also favors the KM process. For example, the preparation of a bid requires cooperation between all the departments. That cooperation arises not from an initiative on the part of the management or a structure more or less favorable to KM but from the very nature of the business processes. The individuals were aware of the advantages to transferring their knowledge, learning and the resulting creation of new knowledge. Feedback between colleagues and learning from experience contributed to the re-examination of the existing knowledge and constituted a constructive exchange.

4.1.5.3. *Mutual adjustment*

Knowledge sharing between colleagues took place, mainly informally, on a daily basis.

4.1.5.4. *Professional characteristics*

However, there were certain profiles which contributed more knowledge than others. Such was the case, for example, of the trainers and the technical support teams manning the "hotline", who had experience of knowledge sharing and, indeed, were accustomed to it. On the other hand, other profiles such as engineers and technicians, who were more accustomed to working independently, were, therefore, less inclined to share their knowledge. This observation is reminiscent of the influence of professional characteristics on knowledge-contribution behavior [MON 08].

IN SUMMARY.– The business process-based structure, the reciprocal interdependence and certain professional characteristics favored KM, which tended to take place by mutual adjustment.

Following the presentation of the results of this initial study, the President and CEO of SCCC authorized us to return to the company for an intensive period of observation (January to December 2007). During the last three months of 2006, when reestablishing contacts in preparation for a return to the field, she initially noted an incomprehensible reticence in relation to the commitment originally given by the President and CEO of SCCC but then realized that S was in the process of a merger with its competitor, N.

4.2. Design of the learning organization SCCC (period of merger with N)

At the start of January 2007, a new company, NSN, was formed. That new company is structured in regions: NSN Tunisia covers the MEA region. During that period of restructuring, stress and uncertainty for the personnel, a target organization was imagined and, then, gradually constructed over the course of 12 months.

4.2.1. Strategy

4.2.1.1. KM: a strategic objective

NSN put training programs in place, requiring every employee to pursue training in accordance with his/her own needs and in negotiation with his/her line manager. That training is verified and evaluated by training reviews every six months. Indeed, in this domain, technology is evolving very quickly, so continued training is necessary. This type of action was undoubtedly implemented to standardize training and eliminate the gaps between the departments.

From the very start, NSN developed awareness-raising activities about the use of shared tools to facilitate the merger and the mixing of the two organizational cultures. This was manifested on the homepage of the NSN intranet by the placement of two links to the respective intranets of S and N, with an identical interface.

4.2.1.2. Hierarchical superiors' support for KM

The company superiors' support for KM and the related tools became firmer during the period of the merger. NSN immediately adopted the KMS developed by S. In addition, the managers, because of their geographic isolation, actually became users of the system themselves.

IN SUMMARY.– The arrival of N as a partner consolidated the strategic objective of KM – particularly because of the firm support of the company directors.

4.2.2. Incentive systems

4.2.2.1. Financial incentive system

NSN decided to greatly decrease the number of expatriates. The result of this was a greater degree of homogeneity in terms of salaries, and a stronger sense of equality.

Career progression, salary increases and bonuses now depend on the quality of the work accomplished.

However, this new financial incentive system has no bearing on the KM and the use of the tools associated therewith.

4.2.2.2. Non-financial incentive systems

4.2.2.2.1. Training

Training policy continues to be advantageous, because N, which is a world leader in the area of mobile networking, encourages the development of skills in both terrestrial and mobile technologies.

4.2.2.2.2. Organizational culture

NSN is dominated by the culture of N – a Nordic culture characterized by less hierarchy, less formal and more spontaneous communication, vigorous marketing and a more aggressive strategy toward the customers.

The new company offers more numerous possibilities for learning and development of skills, through internal job offers, which favors mobility. In addition, the new culture of NSN affords individuals the freedom to act, to construct their own network of contacts, to seek the necessary training and to adopt and appropriate the tools – in other words, to find their own motivation.

4.2.2.2.3. Trust

Trust in the management: the period of transition from SCCC to NSN was difficult for the individuals, who were not at all well informed by their hierarchical superiors. Furthermore, some of those hierarchical superiors prohibited their teams from having any contact with new colleagues from N and from asking questions at informative seminars. Finally, certain hierarchical superiors did not provide their collaborators with the support they needed during the transition, sometimes leaving them without a job, forcing them either to leave the company or to seek their own contacts with the company N, under their own steam, with a view to cooperating and exchanging in order to secure a future job in the new structure.

The restructuring, which was carried out slowly and in secret, accentuated the lack of trust in the management, but this did not affect behaviors in terms of KM or the use of the associated tools.

Trust between colleagues: we observed a greater spirit of helping one another, both within the project teams and between the different teams, probably due to the prevailing atmosphere of major uncertainty during the merger.

In the context of this study, the results found during this phase demonstrate that, when the members lose trust in the management, their trust of one another tends to increase, leading them to cooperate and exchange more between themselves. They develop learning behavior and are more inclined to discover and use KM tools.

4.2.2.2.4. Internal mobility

Internal mobility increased greatly. For some employees, it constitutes an incentive system to learning and the development of knowledge. However, this new incentive system does not apply to all employees, because of the following individual characteristics: marital status and age.

IN SUMMARY.– During the merger, the incentives encouraging KM and the use of KMSs were, primarily, not only the accrued trust among the colleagues but also training, the organizational culture of NSN and, to some extent, mobility.

There was a growing lack of trust in the management, but that did not affect the KM process.

4.2.3. *People*

4.2.3.1. *Individual characteristics*

Individual characteristics such as a person's age, gender, initial training and prior experience do not always seem to have an impact on KM. In fact, during the merger, NSN's culture seemed to absorb the individuals' differences.

4.2.3.2. *National culture*

The theater of operations of NSN is broader (covering the whole MEA area); so, a multicultural mixture emerged, little by little, erasing the initial national cultural duality (German–Tunisian). This mingling, which renders any exchanges richer and more attractive, constitutes a factor for openness toward others and for knowledge sharing.

4.2.3.3. *Language*

English was immediately adopted as NSN's official language, thus breaking down the initial barriers between those who spoke German and those who did not.

IN SUMMARY.– The adoption of English as the sole language and the intermingling of cultures supported KM.

4.2.4. *Technology*

4.2.4.1. *The functions of a KMS*

The KM tools available during the period of the merger were mainly the intranets (of the two companies, S and N), terrestrial and mobile phone technologies and Sharenet-IMS, whose functions are constantly evolving.

4.2.4.1.1. The intranet

The intranet interface includes links to the two intranets of S and N so as to facilitate a quick migration toward an NSN interface. This is one of the main KM tools employed, and its functions have been improved (e-mail, information-seeking and document-mining, storage in the project library, consultation and feedback on previous projects).

4.2.4.1.2. Sharenet-IMS

S's tool, Sharenet-IMS, was immediately adopted by NSN, which standardized it, improving and enriching it. NSN created virtual communities within this tool around different themes, centers of interest and exchanges about the products and working methods.

The Sharenet interface in the tool Sharenet-IMS: This interface was rendered more attractive and efficient (significantly improved response time). In addition, Sharenet is a tool for exchange in the form of discussion forums with the possibility of asking questions or formulating requests and receiving responses from all over the world. The users of that interface deem it interactive and effective, because of its role facilitating the firming up of new contacts and identification of experts in a wide variety of domains. Considered to be a tool for the creation and use of knowledge, based on social processes and interpersonal interactions, this tool places the emphasis on the issue of exchange and, thus, belongs to the category of interactive KMSs based on the network model identified by Alavi and Leidner [ALA 01].

The IMS interface of Sharenet-IMS: The IMS is a data warehouse containing technical and commercial documentation about the products and solutions and a library of the previous projects. According to its users, this tool is characterized by quick updating, access with satisfactory security conditions (login, password, variable levels of authorization depending on the user's profile, etc.) and a good level of support in carrying out professional activities:

– document seeking and finding of projects, updated constantly;

– identifying people whom it would be useful to contact;

– storage of important projects where they are accessible to all;

– provision of the deliverables of a project;

– the quality of the knowledge provided (reliability, accuracy, robustness, etc.).

This tool treats knowledge as an object which can be collected, stored and then reused. It focuses on the problem of storage and belongs to the category of integrative KMSs, based on the warehouse model set out by Alavi and Leidner [ALA 01].

4.2.4.1.3. Other means of communication

In addition to these KM tools, there are various other means of communication: face-to-face contact, e-mail, terrestrial and mobile telephony or indeed SMS, which is very widely used. According to the users of these means of communication, electronic messaging is the quickest way to transfer explicit knowledge between the members of a team working in the same professional area (documents, reports, links, contacts, etc.). This method is becoming increasingly rich, with the passage of time, accumulation of experience and construction of context [LIM 97, REI 04, KAL 06]. The telephone is effective in exchanging urgent, necessary information. SMS, which has been very widely used since the NSN merger, rooted in the culture of N, has become highly effective since the staff all adopted a common language (English) and codes specific to each professional area. In addition, it enables users to contact a person without disturbing him/her when he/she is in a meeting. This means of communication is often felt to be quicker than e-mail, because the recipients of the communication do not always have their workstations available to them (e.g. if they are out of the office).

However, users of these methods note that face-to-face communication prior to the use of e-mail and phone makes the knowledge transfer richer and more effective.

4.2.4.2. *Characteristics of use of KM tools*

It has become an absolute necessity to make use of KM tools. There are no longer any indirect users or limitations to their use.

4.2.4.3. *Ease of use, perceived usefulness and perceived results*

Quite apart from the fact that it is compulsory, the KM tools have become easier to use, and therefore their perceived usefulness and their effects on the work are recognized by their users.

IN SUMMARY.– The arrival of company N as a partner created significant dynamism in relation to KM and communication tools. These devices are used by everyone, and their usefulness is widely recognized.

4.2.5. *Structure*

The experiences of the NSN merger and restructuring for the existing staff were different from one department to another. Thus, during this period, two different types of department can be identified, depending on how quickly they adapted to the new structure. The *Bid Management* and *Technical Bid Management* departments, which switched immediately to the new structure, offer a more propitious example with which to compare it to the old structure of SCCC.

In the newly formed NSN, the function of human resource management carries a greater deal of importance. The role of the Human Resources Department has become more important, given the decrease in the number of hierarchical levels. Line managers work in close collaboration with the human resources directors (HRDs) in the subregions. Hence, the HRD becomes a true partner of the line managers in managing the teams.

4.2.5.1. *Hierarchical levels*

The new structure, NSN, includes fewer hierarchical levels, and a number of positions no longer exist: those of the CEO, CFO and local department heads.

Meanwhile, several new positions have been created. The line manager has direct responsibility for the people whom he/she assigns to projects. Each project is spearheaded by a team leader. Hence, NSN's collaborators are subjected to a matricial structure of the business/project. Once the projects are launched, the teams have direct access to the customer, as does the Sales department, which was not so in the previous structure. Access to the customer has a positive impact on the teams: it encourages them to take more responsibility and improves information handling.

4.2.5.2. *Business processes: versatility*

NSN has developed technical and commercial versatility in both business processes (bid preparation and solution development). Such versatility encourages and enhances KM. This versatility was achieved more or less quickly depending on the team members' professional background.

4.2.5.3. *Mutual adjustment*

Face-to-face communication on site, in the context of the mission, facilitates the transfer of tacit knowledge and the exchange of experiences which are difficult to communicate by telephone or by electronic messaging. Face-to-face contact also proves to be the best and most-effective approach to solving problems relating to language, culture and level of professional experience.

4.2.5.4. *Virtual teams*

Most of the time, the line manager is not at the same location as the teams. This new form of remote management has had a positive impact on KM and the use of the tools associated therewith. Indeed, the fact that the line manager is one step removed encourages the team members to rely on one another, to help each other, to exchange and create new contacts. Hence, knowledge is created by socialization and by internalization. The fact that the individuals have to assume greater responsibility increases their confidence in their own knowledge and encourages them to help their colleagues by sharing that knowledge. It is also worth noting that the virtual presence of the hierarchical superiors reduces the divisions previously seen between the departments and tends to promote uniformity in the relations between the employees and the hierarchical superiors in the company.

IN SUMMARY.– The new structure encourages KM and the use of the tools associated therewith. However, mutual adjustment always proves to be a useful strategy for the exchange and sharing of knowledge.

4.3. Design of the learning organization NSN (post-merger)

4.3.1. *Strategy*

4.3.1.1. *KM: a strategic objective*

NSN's strategy centers on the development of skills and the use of dedicated KM tools. The objectives are set and revised twice a year, by a performance-evaluation process called *Personal Development Performance* (PDP). Learning is an integral part of the objectives for each employee to achieve, in accordance with the following principle: 70% of learning is done "on the job", 20% through coaching, monitoring and networking, and 10% through conventional training. It is on these principles that the company relies when developing the individuals' skill levels. Consequently, the culture favored by NSN is geared more toward interaction and exchange between individuals, whether face to face or remotely through the use of tools.

Before the objectives for the next year are decided upon, an annual performance review takes place, measuring how closely the goals have been adhered to over the past year in terms of KM. The objective of cost reduction leads to lowering of travel expenses and the reduction in the number of meetings and face-to-face training sessions. However, the negative effects entailed by this objective are compensated by the positive effects of another – to promote universal use of KM tools, training and remote communication.

4.3.1.2. *Support of the company directors for KM*

In the MEA, the regional head of skills development is based in Dubai. Hence, close collaboration between the line managers, the Human Resources Department and the head of skills development is needed in order to define and implement a coherent training policy.

In addition, as almost all teams are now run remotely, the line managers and team leaders support KM tools and do, themselves, make use of them regularly.

IN SUMMARY.– KM is a strategic objective which is realized, that is implemented, by managers under the control of the Human Resources Department and the regional head of skills development. Specially designed KM tools are used by all project teams.

4.3.2. *Incentive systems*

4.3.2.1. *Financial incentive system*

Numerous improvements have been made as compared to the financial incentive system in place previously. The current system is felt to be fairer because the status of "expatriate" has been eliminated. At NSN, in keeping with the matrix structure, salaries and financial benefits are attributed as a function of the evaluation not only from the line manager but also from the team leaders. The appraisal of each individual is supported by a new online tool, which allows anybody – in addition to his/her line manager – to invite all the team leaders with whom he/she has worked to contribute to its appraisal. The new evaluation system is perceived by the employees as being more transparent and more objective.

In spite of these significant changes, the financial incentive system is not always of crucial importance for the KM process.

4.3.2.2. *Non-financial incentive system*

4.3.2.2.1. Training

NSN Tunisia now has its own training body. Training continues to be an important satisfaction factor for the individuals. The content of the training directly supports the structure. Indeed, besides the technical content, in the domains of terrestrial and mobile telephony, new training is being offered. This new training is intended to be the corollary of the matricial structure, virtual teams (time management and stress management) and versatility (improved sales capacities).

The very form of the available training has also diversified. In addition to conventional training, it is now possible to train on the job with the help of colleagues, in the form of coaching or networking with KM and remote-communication tools. The information provided to individuals about the available training has become much better. Thus, each individual is informed in advance by e-mail of the future organization of training sessions (topics, date, place and format). It is then up to the individual to confirm whether or not he/she will participate in that training. In all cases, a detailed breakdown of the content of the training can be found on the company intranet.

NSN provides varied and significant resources for training, improvement of knowledge and development of skills. However, it is the individuals alone who must take the initiative to take up the opportunity to train and choose the modes and content of training.

Finally, the decrease of face-to-face training has had a variable impact depending on the individual characteristics of the team members.

4.3.2.2.2. Organizational culture

The employees seem to be motivated by the organizational culture and the quality of the working environment at NSN. Indeed, with the creation of the new NSN structure, more relaxed and less formal relations than before have been established, both between individuals and between individuals and their hierarchical superiors. Hence, now, the hierarchical superiors are available at any time by phone, e-mail or indeed on discussion forums and blogs. Similarly, the disappearance of the obligatory dress code and the development of informal address ("tu" form of address, rather than the honorific "vous") have contributed to the establishment of an atmosphere of trust between the team members and their supervisors. NSN's company culture seems more favorable to knowledge creation and knowledge sharing, because it involves a greater degree of responsibility on the part of the individuals, encourages the use of dedicated KM tools, favors mobility and humanizes the relations between team members and between the team members and their hierarchical superiors. However, the potential effects of NSN's company culture only become a personal reality when national culture is erased and individual characteristics are adapted to the new company culture. Certain people who are heavily imbued with Tunisian national culture, who generally have numerous family constraints, have a preference for stable jobs and do not adapt well to NSN's culture, which offers less stability – geographically (frequent travel for work) and professionally (restructuring every six months). Other people, who are less impregnated with the national culture, notably because of studies abroad, because of their age and because they have fewer family constraints, are better able to adapt to the culture of NSN.

4.3.2.2.3. Trust

Remote teams and the intensive use of tools have meant that the team members have become more autonomous. Trust between the team members and between different teams no longer seems absolutely necessary for the development and sharing of knowledge.

Furthermore, although relations between the employees and the directors have improved, the issue of trust in the management still does not appear to have an impact on the KM and the use of the associated tools.

4.3.2.2.4. Mobility

During the merger, the majority of employees seemed to have taken the principles of mobility on board. After the merger, we observed multiple cases where employees refused mobility. Some such refusals were accepted by the line managers. In other cases, the collaborators had to leave the company. On the other hand, employees who have truly adopted the culture of NSN express a clear preference for mobility in order to acquire international experience.

IN SUMMARY.– The remote training, the culture of NSN and the mobility promote the development of KM and the use of its tools. However, this new form of training, that new culture and the mobility do not seem to suit certain collaborators, who have difficulty adapting to the new working conditions.

4.3.3. *People*

4.3.3.1. Individual characteristics

Individual characteristics such as age and gender do not always have a significant influence on KM and the appropriation of KM tools.

4.3.3.2. *National culture*

Tunisian national culture is less well suited to NSN culture than it was to SCCC culture. This being the case, certain individuals who are profoundly attached to their national culture have experienced difficulty in adapting to the culture of NSN and, therefore, to the KM process which is part of that culture.

4.3.3.3. *Language*

English has become the official language of NSN. Its impact on KM is no longer as significant as it was before the merger.

4.3.3.4. *Level of experience and nature of the knowledge exchanged*

It has been noted that, when the knowledge being exchanged is complex in nature, it is nearly impossible for two people, with unequal levels of professional experience, to conduct an exchange using tools. In this case, face-to-face contact is absolutely necessary.

The detection of this phenomenon during the final period of observation is linked to the generalized implementation of versatility, which involves more marked unequal levels of experience in exchanges.

IN SUMMARY.– After the merger, the effects of Tunisian national culture had indirect negative repercussions for KM. Furthermore, with an unequal level of experience in the profession, the exchange and sharing of complex knowledge is only possible face to face.

4.3.4. Technology

4.3.4.1. *Functions of the KM tools and their evolution*

All the available tools are integrated into a single interface. There is no separation between NSN's KM tools. Those tools are all connected to one another. Such is the case, for instance, with Sharenet-IMS, which can be accessed automatically from the company intranet. Indeed, when searching on the intranet, users are automatically rerouted to the Sharenet-IMS tools, even without wanting to be.

4.3.4.1.1. NSN intranet

Characterized by the richness of its content and the extent of its use, NSN's intranet, which was created in the wake of the merger, gradually came to replace the two links to the intranets of S and N. To begin with, the individuals in NSN now have more detailed, continually updated information available, about all the topics linked to the company and the professions. Next, those individuals are informed by e-mail as soon as any new information is published on the intranet. In addition, it is possible to consult RSS feeds on the main events occurring in the company, in the form of video of the meetings or events.

The intranet is fed by the service *MEA Internal Communication*, which is responsible for internal communication in that region.

Access to that tool is granted to all NSN's collaborators. However, different user profiles have been defined so that each individual only has access to the information that is useful for his/her work.

4.3.4.1.2. Sharenet-IMS

The Sharenet run by the company S had very limited access and archiving. Today, archiving is centralized, usage is generalized and obligatory. Numerous improvements have been made to the tool Sharenet-IMS since the creation of the new structure, NSN. These improvements pertain to the tool's functions and its use. Sharenet-IMS is a content-management professional software package facilitating storage and exchange in satisfactory security conditions.

The main functions offered by Sharenet-IMS are:

– access to the intranet;

– workflow management;

– management of virtual project teams;

– management of e-communities;

– integration into the environment (Microsoft Office);

– management of document configuration;

– online help for use.

Various profiles are managed: information user, information provider and content and information-access manager:

– the profile "information user" corresponds to editing and downloading rights over the information generated by Sharenet-IMS but without the opportunity to update that information;

– the profile "information provider" includes the rights associated with the previous profile and the rights to update the database associated with the application Sharenet-IMS;

– the profile "content and information-access manager" corresponds to the responsibility of administration of the software's maintenance.

The implementation of these functions in the context of the project teams are illustrated by two examples:

– *Workspace, project space:* The project manager has the option to create a workspace for the project. Thus, that workspace is exclusively dedicated to the project. He/she assigns access rights to all the team members so that everyone can access and work on the content, add and exchange about everything concerning the state of advancement of the project. As the team members are not necessarily all in the same place or even in the same country, that workspace is the main point of meeting, research and exchange about the project. That space may contain large files, which are problematic to send *via* e-mail. It has helped resolve a certain number of the disadvantages of previous tools;

– *e-Communities:* There are numerous e-communities on various subjects relating to the domain of activity. They are classified by theme, region, activity, product, etc. Users need only click on a theme, and they obtain a description of the theme in question, the members, the creator or the person who is in charge of that community, information on how to access and become a member of the community. Today, all the staffs receive informative e-mails about everything that happens on Sharenet: creation of new e-communities, online training, creation of a group, event, etc.

4.3.4.1.3. New communication tools

New communication tools have been put in place – primarily Voice over IP (VoIP) and telecom tools, which serve to support the KM tools:

– *WebX:* a tool designed for remote conferences and meetings. Users need only create a meeting on WebX and invite participants, by sending them electronic invites. The participants can consult various types of documents and interact, posing questions in writing or orally. They also have the possibility to access the meeting leader's workstation and tweak the presentation in accordance with the access rights he/she has granted them. Finally, the meeting's content is posted on Sharenet in the form of a document or video so that those people who were not present can consult it. *WebX* facilitates an exchange between multiple people, whereas Netmeeting is limited to an exchange between two people;

– *Tellco*: a teleconferencing tool;

– *My room*: a tool for booking a meeting room online;

– *S View*: this tool archives the different online training sessions and the documentation pertaining to those sessions;

– *Voice Conference*: this tool enables users to run a video-conference, with IP technology;

– *Corina*: this application allows users to use any type of network to connect to the company intranet from their laptop computer.

Today, mobile telephony technologies play an important role not only in supporting the process of KM but also in the daily workings of NSN. This role manifests itself in an increased use of SMS. All of NSN's staffs have mobile phones with multiples integrated applications, meaning they can access electronic messages at any time, from anywhere.

4.3.4.2. *Characteristics of use of dedicated KM tools*

The use of KM tools is obligatory and is generalized for the project teams.

4.3.4.3. *Ease of use, perceived usefulness and perceived results*

KM tools and communication methods have become indispensable for the performance of all professional duties. Such tools have become easier to use. The perceived usefulness and perceived results of these tools are considerable, in that it is nearly impossible for any collaborator to work without using them.

IN SUMMARY.– We have seen great dynamism surrounding KM through the development of the associated tools and communication tools, alongside the fact that their use has become widespread and obligatory at all levels of the company.

4.3.5. *Structure*

After the merger, the number of staff on the books at NSN in Tunisia dropped from 202 to 114 people. The whole structure has changed: today, NSN is completely different from SCCC. Before, there were the parent company and subsidiary branches in different countries and regions, and any decision always needed to be taken by the parent company. Today, NSN operates in regions and subregions which are more independent.

4.3.5.1. *Hierarchical levels*

There are three categories of managers:

– The *solid-line manager* is the direct supervisor. Each person in the organization depends on a solid-line manager, who is his/her professional manager;

– The *dotted-line manager* is the project manager. He/she oversees one or more projects. Any person working on a project is attached to a dotted-line manager;

– The *second-line manager* is the line manager of the line manager, who is also part of the "solid-line" professional hierarchy.

NSN is also organized on the basis of the customer. Thus, in Tunisia, there are two customer liaisons: one for Tunisie Télécom and the other for Tunisiana.

Finally, the structure of NSN, in project teams, is matricial with three dimensions: profession/project/customer. This matricial structure is fairly complex, in that an engineer can, at the same moment, depend on his/her line manager, one or more dotted-line managers and one or more customer liaisons.

4.3.5.2. *Business processes*

The professional processes (bid preparation and solution development) and the activities involved in these processes remained the same. The responsibilities evolved with the remote matricial structure. This new structure and the tools changed the way in which activities were carried out.

4.3.5.3. *Mutual adjustment*

Mutual adjustment now involves all sorts of communication tools, and there has been a marked decrease in traditional face-to-face contact. This tendency toward remote work and virtual relations to the detriment of meeting in the flesh does not seem to be to everybody's tastes.

4.3.5.4. *Versatility*

Solely technical profiles have disappeared from the spectrum. All engineers must, in addition to their technical specialty, possess commercial skills. Such versatility fits in with NSN's customer-oriented approach.

Certain specialties, such as IT, have greater difficulty in acquiring commercial skills and becoming versatile.

Generally, versatility makes collaborators more able to exchange and share knowledge.

IN SUMMARY.– The complex structure (matricial and virtual) makes KM tools absolutely indispensable. Increasingly, mutual adjustment involves the use of technical communication devices, and versatility encourages knowledge exchange and sharing.

4.4. Overview of the three phases

Table 4.1 presents the results over the three phases. There are a number of comments that can be made.

First, six elements in our model appeared to have little or no impact on the process of KM and the use of its tools. Two of these pertain to the incentive system and the other four to personal characteristics.

The financial incentive system, which is always pointed out by Galbraith in the different versions of his "star model [GAL 73, GAL 77, GAL 02b], and trust in the management, have no discernible effect on KM. The company culture and training seem to have a greater motivating effect on people than do financial aspects. The absence of trust in the management does not preclude the other form of trust – trust in one's colleagues; quite the opposite, in fact: during the period of the merger in particular, trust between colleagues compensated, to some extent, for the mistrust built up toward the management. In addition, the target population, essentially made up of engineers and experts, perhaps has less need to rely on trust in the management to carry out their allotted activities.

The characteristics of age, gender, hierarchical level and previous experience of knowledge exchange, which are highlighted in the literature on KM, play no part in our case study. Regarding the age and gender, the population of the sample studied here is fairly typical of a multinational in the telecom sector: it is composed mainly of men aged between 25 and 40 years. Thus, it seems difficult to observe differences arising from these characteristics. Hierarchical level has no influence on KM behaviors, and in terms of that metric, the sample includes people of several different hierarchical levels. No differences regarding the characteristic of previous experience of exchange were detected, in that mutual adjustment and trust between colleagues were intense. On the other hand, we observed the emergence of a characteristic linked to prior experience: prior experience of the profession, in the third phase.

Three elements came to light, which were not defined in our original model. Mobility and versatility come into being during the merger and have a positive effect on the process of KM and the use of the associated tools. Then, in the third phase, they have a contradictory effect (indicated by + and – in Table 4.1). These are elements which are deliberately assimilated from the culture of N. Mobility constitutes an incentive system for the development of KM, and versatility is a structural condition of KM. We believe that, during the period of uncertainty and stress which was the merger, people were unable to react to the influence of the organizational culture. In the post-merger period, when everybody was able to manifest his/her agreement or disagreement with the idea of mobility and reticence or openness to versatility, the effects on KM appeared to be contradictory.

The third emerging and contradictory element occurs during the third phase: professional experience; when there are different levels of experience present, knowledge exchange and sharing can only take place by mutual adjustment. However, in this third phase, many remote communication tools are put in place to facilitate a mutual adjustment without the need for face-to-face contact. Yet, it is not always possible to substitute tools for face-to-face exchanges, whether because the nature of the knowledge to be exchanged is too complex or because the people involved are not sufficiently comfortable with the new tools. Such non-substitution of the tools would account for the adverse effect on KM.

Components: Factors identified from the literature	SCCC (before merger), 10 interviews	Merger S and N (during merger), 35 interviews	NSN (Post-merger), 15 interviews
Strategy			
KM: strategic objective	++ (7) and – (3)	+ + (35)	+ + + (15)
Support from the directors	+ (2) and – – (8)	+ + (35)	+ + + (15)
Incentive systems			
Financial			
Non-financial			
Training	+ + (10)	+ + (35)	+ + (11) and – (4)
Organizational culture			
Trust in the management	+ + (10)	++ (35)	+ + (11) and – (4)
Trust in colleagues	+ (7)	+ + + (35)	
		Mobility + (29)	+ (9) and – (6)
People			
Age			
Gender			
Hierarchical level			
Previous experience of exchange			
National culture			+ (10) and – (5)
Language	+ (6) and – (4)	+ (35)	+ (15)
			Professional experience +(12) and –(3)
Technology			
Use	+ (3) and – – (7)	+ (35)	+ + (15)
Ease of use	+ (3) and – – (7)	+ (29)	+ + (15)
Perceived usefulness	+ (3) and – – (7)	+ (29)	+ + (15)
Perceived results	+ (3) and – – (7)	+ (29)	+ + (15)

Structure			
Organigram	+ (3) and – (7)	+ (29)	+ + (11) and – (4)
Interdependence	+ (10)	+ (35)	+ (15)
Professional characteristics	+ (6) and – (4)	+ (24) and – (11)	+ (12) and – (3)
Mutual adjustment	+ + + (10)	+ + (35)	+ (10) and – (5)
		Versatility + (29)	+ (10) and – (5)
		Virtuality + (29)	+ (11) and – (4)

Table 4.1. *Results from the three phases, compared against the factors derived from the literature and the emergent factors*

Finally, two components of our model – strategy and technology – have an increasing positive effect on the development of KM. Thus, gradually KM has become a real strategic objective, for which there are ample tools in place.

5

Emergence of a New Organizational Design

This chapter discusses the results of the case study, hinging on three subjects:

– the design of the learning organization (section 5.1);

– the impact of culture on knowledge management (KM) (section 5.2);

– the management of knowledge boundaries (section 5.3).

5.1. Emergence of a design of the learning organization

Five domains of the learning organization have been identified: strategy, incentive systems, people, technology and structure. These different domains of organizational design must be harmoniously aligned with one another, in order to send a clear and consistent message to the company's employees. Illustrations drawn from the cross-cutting case study demonstrate the consistency or inconsistency of the design of the learning organization.

5.1.1. *Flexibility through integrative devices*

In the eyes of Galbraith [GAL 94, GAL 00b, GAL 02a, GAL 02b], "processes" provide an organization with flexibility by way of a network of interactions. Four categories of processes, or means of integration of the units, can be applied: informal groups, artifact-based coordination, creation of integration manager jobs and, finally, the construction of a matricial organization. NSN has implemented all means of integration in its KM activities:

– coordination based on informal groups by the creation of virtual communities (e-communities);

– artifact-based coordination (the artifacts in question being knowledge management systems (KMSs) and communication tools);

– attribution of the role of integrating managers to the regional heads of skills development;

– implementation of a matricial structure.

NSN can be considered a flexible organization. In all likelihood, this flexibility (a means) is geared toward reactivity (an end) in a sector which is unstable and highly competitive.

5.1.2. Consistency/inconsistency in regard to the domain "strategy"

A significant body of literature has showed that the success of a KM approach lies in the exercising of strategy by the organization, which views this process and the tools supporting it as an important objective [GIN 99, HOL 00, LES 00, KOS 01, JEN 03, MAN 98]. The results of the study presented here have demonstrated that this necessary condition is not sufficient. In terms of strategy, execution is crucially important. Publicizing one's objectives does not ensure they will be achieved, and the fact that KMSs are available does not mean that they will necessarily be used.

Such was the case during the first phase of the study. SCCC was exercising a KM strategy which did not have the support of the managers, and the available KMS suffered from a number of technical and functional imperfections. It was used very randomly and rather sparingly. In this case, we see not only an inconsistency between one element of the strategy (the objective) and another element – the support of the directors – but also a second inconsistency with another domain of the design of the learning organization: the technology.

During the other two phases, KM was consolidated as a strategic objective, thanks to a stated policy of human resources and skill management, involving the managers. The KMS was continuously improved, and it became more widely used and standardized. The managers were all the more supportive of the use of KMSs when it proved necessary, in the context of remote or virtual project teams. This observation demonstrates three aspects of consistency between the components of the model presented herein. First, the learning organization aligns KM with its strategy. Second, it aligns human resources management and technology with KM. Finally, these combined factors, along with the organizational structure, enable us define incentive systems for the managers. The observations made during the case study join those of numerous authors who have shown the important role played by the support of the company directors, including resource allocation, leadership and the provision of training opportunities [DAV 98b, HOL 00, JEN 00, YU 04].

5.1.3. Consistency/inconsistency in regard to the "incentive systems" domain

Trust between colleagues, which was present throughout the three phases, had a varying effect on the development of KM.

In the SCCC phase, the trust between colleagues led to an overly rigid and hierarchical structure. The members of the project teams, considered to be subordinates, have very little familiarity with the customers. The development of "customer knowledge" by the project teams was curbed.

The context of the merger, characterized by instability, uncertainty and lack of trust in the management, brought the individuals closer together. Mutual assistance and knowledge sharing developed, based on much stronger trust between colleagues.

After the merger, the new structure, which is highly flexible and formed of well-equipped remote teams, no longer seems to have to rely on trust in colleagues for the development of knowledge. The incentive systems activated during that phase have contradictory effects on KM. For example, remote training tools, organizational culture and mobility do not serve as incentives for everybody.

5.1.4. Consistency/inconsistency in regard to the "technology" domain

The results of the case study show the improvement in KM practices over the course of the three phases examined. This improvement manifested itself by the evolution of the existing KMSs (intranet, Sharenet-IMS), the establishment of new KMSs (remote working tools) and the wider adoption of the use of those tools.

During the first phase, the existence of a KMS was not sufficient to encourage its widespread use or to develop knowledge sharing. The other domains of the conception of the organizational design of SCCC constituted obstacles to KM, which were such that the KMS was not maintained and kept up to date.

During the period of the merger, these obstacles were gradually removed. The use of technology, in the form of the KMSs installed and operated, developed and eventually became widespread after the merger. When the new organizational design of NSN was implemented, the use of the technology (KMS) no longer encountered any obstacles and developed fully.

5.1.5. Consistency/inconsistency in regard to the "structure" domain

The hierarchical structure of SCCC represented an obstacle to KM and the use of KM tools. Given that SCCC's hierarchical pyramid was in keeping with other domains of the organizational design – which also constituted a hindrance to KM – the mutual adjustment in the teams and between teams (a condition which is favorable to the development of knowledge) was not sufficient to fully develop the process of KM. The different elements of the new NSN structure constitute ambivalent conditions for KM. However, this process developed better than during the SCCC era. Each structural option has its own advantages and disadvantages. In the view of Galbraith [GAL 02b], it is possible to remedy the disadvantages of the structure by acting on the other components of the organizational design. From our point of view, it is the modes of integration (which are highly sophisticated at NSN) which counteract the ambivalence of the effects of the structure on knowledge development. These modes include e-communities, KMSs notably supporting communication and coordination, the regional heads of skills development and the matricial structure.

5.2. Emergence of a new organizational design in view of the impact of culture

When analyzing the results of the case study in its three phases, we noted that, once the merger had reached a sufficient level of maturity and a more stable organizational atmosphere had been established, some of the organizational conditions acting on the development of KM, identified as part of the model, became variable, contradictory or ambivalent. It later became apparent that the reason behind this ambivalence was the impact of a threefold cultural profile (national culture, organizational culture and professional culture).

The individuals' behavior toward learning and knowledge sharing is influenced by the professional characteristics of the roles they fulfill in the organizations. Similarly, whether or not a new culture is adopted is greatly influenced by the national culture. In the case study, the employees had different responses in adopting the *modus operandi* and new professional practices of NSN, whose culture and strategy are heavily oriented toward remote work and the use of tools. Therefore, the success of a KM program at NSN is partly determined by the professional culture, organizational culture and the employees' national culture. These results confirm the conclusions of numerous authors, who believe that individuals' motivation to share their knowledge is linked to the belief structures, values, standards and practices accepted within the organization [SZU 04, CHI 07, SAC 07, NAY 08, RAV 11, JON 11, ALM 14]. These institutional structures constitute "cultures" including the national culture, organizational culture, organizational climate, team atmosphere, organizational subcultures and unit cultures [KIN 08].

For his part, Ruggles [RUG 98], analyzing the results obtained from an inquiry carried out by Ernst and Young on the basis of 431 European and American organizations, concluded that culture is the most important determining factor for KM. Cultural barriers are among the most significant obstacles to effective KM [MCD 01, MCC 04, RIE 05, ROS 07, SAC 07, BAR 09, CHM 12].

Consequently, culture is both important and problematic for KM. According to King [KIN 06], even though beliefs about the significant influence of organizational culture on the process of KM are well established, it is nonetheless true that in turn, KM, by way of its practices, influences the culture, organizational atmosphere and team atmosphere. Indeed, the hypotheses, values and artifacts making up the culture may be impacted by new knowledge. This is organizational learning, which transforms practices into routines which, when incorporated into the organizational atmosphere and culture, guide individuals' behavior [LEV 88]. In other words, culture and KM exert reciprocal influences on one another, and the practices and results arising from the KM process are iteratively incorporated into the culture, becoming integrated into it.

Thus, the artifacts and values of the organizational culture or organizational atmosphere are influenced by the results of the KM process. This process can be seen as one of the methods that facilitate explicit development of these artifacts and values. Furthermore, the influence of organizational culture on KM may be positive or negative. Indeed, there are practices of organizational culture – such as sharing, openness or trust – which lead to favorable behaviors contributing positively to KM [ONE 07, BEC 08, HOL 10]. On the other hand, other practices such as individualism and competition between individuals give rise to unfavorable behaviors which can cause KM to fail [KIN 01, HUS 12, WEN 13].

The results of this study confirm that not only can culture influence the process of KM but also the practices implemented as part of that process can, in turn, contribute to the construction of a professional culture and to the consolidation of an organizational culture. Thus, organizational actors may very well be united by KM practices whatever their origins in terms of national culture. Similarly, the fact that culture and KM exert reciprocal influences on one another explains the variability, contradiction and ambivalence noted in the empirical results found.

5.3. Emergence of a new organizational design when faced with knowledge boundaries

This section analyzes the results obtained in terms of knowledge boundaries and boundary objects. To begin with, we shall look at the management of knowledge boundaries and then apply it to the case study at hand.

5.3.1. *Knowledge boundary management*

From his work on KM, Carlile [CAR 02a, CAR 04] identified three relational properties of knowledge situated at the boundaries of different domains of knowledge: difference, dependency and novelty [CAR 03]. Difference relates to the quantity and/or type of knowledge accumulated by the different actors involved in a project. Without dependency, the difference between the knowledge held by two actors has no influence. Novelty characterizes the intensity of the changes affecting the context – that is the dependencies and differences between the actors involved in a shared project.

Management of knowledge boundaries is necessary to facilitate the knowledge sharing required to achieve the common objectives of the project team.

Carlile [CAR 04] distinguishes three types of knowledge boundaries: syntactic, semantic and pragmatic. He outlines three possible approaches to manage them effectively.

The syntactic boundary is characterized by stability and mastery of the differences and dependencies between the organizational actors. According to Carlile, knowledge transfer is the most appropriate approach to deal with syntactical boundaries. Such an approach – a so-called information-handling-oriented approach – is based on the development of a common lexicon (language) to share and evaluate the knowledge at the boundaries.

The transition between the syntactical boundary and the semantic boundary takes place when the novelty renders certain dependencies and differences or certain interpretations ambiguous. To manage semantic boundaries, Carlile [CAR 04] suggests a translational approach (the "interpretative" approach), to create common interpretations which constitute appropriate means to share and evaluate the knowledge at the boundaries.

The passage from a semantic boundary to a pragmatic boundary takes place when significant novelty causes conflicting interests between the actors. Those interests constitute obstacles to sharing and evaluation of knowledge at the boundaries. Indeed, in the presence of conflicting interests, the knowledge developed in one domain often has negative consequences for the others, manifested in the form of costs incurred for each of the actors belonging to the domains involved. Because of these costs, the actors are less willing to effect these changes, in spite of the presence of a significant "degree of novelty". According to Carlile [CAR 04], the management of pragmatic boundaries is based on a transformation method – known as the policy-based approach – which facilitates the development of common interests by transforming the actor's conflicting interests and knowledge.

Those common interests constitute adequate means to share and evaluate the knowledge at the boundaries.

Note that sharing of knowledge at the boundaries involves the creation of boundary objects shared by the different organizational actors involved in a project.

The discussion of the results obtained in light of the research framework set forth by Carlile [CAR 04] entails answering the following questions for each of the three phases of study:

– What are the characteristics of the knowledge boundaries observed?

– What are the boundary objects created to facilitate knowledge sharing at those boundaries?

– What is the position of the research model presented herein in relation to the research framework proposed by Carlile [CAR 04] to facilitate knowledge sharing at the boundaries of the domains of specialty?

5.3.2. *Design of the learning organization in the face of knowledge boundaries*

Before attempting to answer these questions, it must be remarked upon that the research framework proffered by Carlile [CAR 04] is appropriate for analysis of the results found by this study. First, the collected data pertain to project teams which each have objectives to achieve, shared by all of their members. Second, the members of the project teams in question carry out mutually complementary activities. The result is that these organizational actors are at once different (because of the specialist knowledge they hold) and dependent (because they have to contribute to the realization of shared goals). Such is the case, for instance, with engineers belonging to the technical support team, trainers and actors carrying out the activities of a business process.

Hence, there are problems of knowledge sharing at the boundaries between the domains of specialty, which need to be resolved in order for each project team to achieve its objectives. Finally, the stability of the differences and dependencies between the members of a project team can be compromised by at least two types of novelty: endogenous and/or exogenous. Endogenous novelties are inherent to the specific characteristics of the project – that is the activities performed by the members of a project team, the resources mobilized in the project or indeed the customers' requirements. Exogenous novelties often result from a major change in the organizational context, such as the merger between S and N. The characteristics of the field observed suggest that, whichever period of study one looks at, all three types of knowledge boundaries may exist, depending on the intensity of the inherent novelty of the projects under way.

However, the knowledge boundaries during the start of the merger between S and N and the creation of the new company (NSN) can actually be viewed as being mainly pragmatic in nature. This is due mainly to an exogenous novelty – in this case, the merger – and the resulting uncertainty of context, having jeopardized the stability of the differences and dependencies between the members of the project teams. At this stage of the merger, different or conflicting interests emerged from the actors' uncertainty as to the evolution of their positions and their continuing future at the newly formed NSN.

Similarly, we can consider that the first period of the case study at hand is associated with syntactic knowledge boundaries, due to the lack of significant novelty inherent to the projects. Thus, during each of the three periods studied, all three of the approaches to knowledge boundaries management proposed by Carlile [CAR 04] are present. What sets these three periods apart are the means brought to bear – that is the role of the conditions of development of the KM identified by the theoretical model at hand and aspects linked to the different prevalent cultures in the company. The conditions of development of effective KM represent the basic instruments for boundaries management approaches proposed by Carlile [CAR 04], in that these approaches aim at the creation of common knowledge shared by the members of a team and necessary to achieve the goal of the project on which the team is working. In other words, these conditions are the determining success factors for Carlile's approaches [CAR 04].

In the continuation of this section, we discuss the contribution of each condition identified by the model presented here to Carlile's [CAR 04] approaches, in light of the results of this study. The description of the contribution of culture and KMSs will supplement the analysis. The KM strategy constituted a crucial factor in the formation of intentions to contribute to the success of the KM program and to the sharing of knowledge within NSN. Indeed, the KM strategy was the subject of mass communication in NSN during the second and third phases of the study, but that campaign of communication was also accompanied by increased use of KMSs and the introduction of remote communication tools at all levels, including the management levels. Thus, the strategy contributed to the successful implementation of knowledge–boundaries–management approaches in NSN. The same was not true for SCCC, because of the management's insufficient involvement.

Incentivization by training with the new technologies played a positive role in the success of KM, in each of the periods of the study. Like any incentive system, access to training can help reduce employees' aversion to sharing their knowledge and their fear that, if they do so, they may lose their power or their benefits. To begin with, access to training facilitates negotiation between the team members when conflicting interests arise and, thus, contributes to the success of the pragmatic approach to boundaries management in an unstable context. In addition, training constitutes an effective way to help the employees construct a common lexicon and common interpretations, which will reduce their differences. However, whilst the impact of access to training on the establishment of a knowledge management strategy was positive during the first and second periods of the study, the same was not true in the third period. Indeed, during this period, the development of tool-supported remote training, with a view to reducing costs, actually demotivated some of the team members who were more in favor of the conventional, face-to-face training methods used at SCCC. The evolution of the training approach aroused conflicting interests in these employees, in addition to resistance to change, and extra instability of their differences and dependencies with their colleagues. The new mode of training, which represented a major novelty for them, threw up new barriers to knowledge sharing. These barriers were able to be broken down by the introduction of other incentives or other techniques facilitating negotiation such as change management. We can also analyze the fact that a new mode of training will be negatively perceived by a portion of the staff, based on Carlile's [CAR 04] remark about the negative effects of knowledge, on the effectiveness of his proposed approaches, when that knowledge is imposed by an actor who holds a high level of power. During the second and third periods, that actor was the management of NSN, acting through the design of the structure and that of the organizational culture.

This analysis is also valid in regard to the effects of language on KM during the first period. Indeed, on the one hand, the language constituted a means of integration, which facilitated knowledge sharing for those employees who did have a command of German, and on the other hand, it was a barrier to knowledge sharing for all the other employees. This double-edged effect of language is another illustration of a case where an actor holding significant power imposes knowledge on the other actors involved in a project. In the present case, these actors are the management and the German expatriates at SCCC, who made no effort to master any language other than their own mother tongue, which they imposed on all employees as being the only means by which to share knowledge. Thus, the employees who were unable to integrate the imposed knowledge – that is the German language – were not able to effectively contribute to knowledge sharing in SCCC. This is a manifestation of the negative effect of national culture on the results of Carlile's [CAR 04] approaches at SCCC. Put differently, the choice of German as the official working language by the management and the expatriates can be analyzed as a negative effect of national culture on KM. The fact that, at NSN, the official working language is English can be considered a contribution to the pragmatic approach to management of knowledge boundaries during the second and third periods of the study, characterized by significant degrees of novelty, both exogenous and endogenous. The negative effect of Tunisian national culture on

KM appears to be less marked in NSN. The results drawn from second period constitute an illustration of Carlile's pragmatic approach [CAR 04]. Indeed, other interests, such as the wish to keep their jobs, arose for NSN's employees, who, therefore, relegated their attachment to their national culture to the background.

With regard to the third period, when the merger had matured somewhat, the negative effect of national culture on the use of Carlile's [CAR 04] approaches was insignificant, because those employees who were deeply attached to Tunisian national culture eventually left NSN.

During the first period of the study, the structure of SCCC was a hindrance to the efficiency of KM. Indeed, the importance of the number of hierarchical levels, alongside the insufficient involvement by the managers, multiplied and intensified the differences between employees, making it risky to implement a KM program, whatever the approach used to manage the knowledge boundaries. This negative effect was tempered during the second and third periods of this study, thanks to the decrease in number of hierarchical levels, bringing the employees and their management closer together, thereby encouraging dialog and negotiation. The complexity caused by the matricial structure of NSN and the decrease in face-to-face relations because of the virtualization of the teams are negative factors which have been compensated in a pragmatic boundary-management approach by integration devices [CAR 04].

The improvement of the KM process from one period to the next, both in terms of the methods and practices and in terms of the tools, contributed to the success of that process, particularly in NSN, regardless of the approach used for the management of the knowledge boundaries. KMSs played a twofold role: the first role pertains to the technical support that they provided for the collection, storage and restitution of the knowledge; the second is linked to the concept of boundary objects defined by Star [STA 89] and Carlile [CAR 02a]. To begin with, the tools contribute to the construction of boundary objects incorporating the shared knowledge generated by the implementation of knowledge boundaries management approaches. The designs, prototypes and shared lexicon and examples of such objects, constructed with the help of the KM tools. Moreover, the tools alter the behaviors of the team members and the management with regard to knowledge sharing, by demystifying certain aspects of KM and reducing aversions and concerns. Such is the case with the hierarchical leaders of NSN who, themselves, became users of KMSs and were, therefore, more involved in the establishment of a KM strategy and more concerned with the success of such a strategy. The new behaviors favorable to KM on the part of NSN's employees and their hierarchical superiors can be considered boundary objects. Finally, having become inextricably associated with KM at NSN, and evolving as a function of the approaches implemented to manage the knowledge boundaries, KMSs themselves became boundary objects in the second and third periods of the study.

Another important aspect of KM pertains to culture and its threefold effect. As highlighted in the previous chapters 1, 2, and 4, three cultural profiles may exist in an organization (national, organizational and professional cultures) and influence KM. In turn, the KM process influences the culture, and facilitates the construction of a professional culture and the consolidation of organizational culture within and between project teams. This results in common KM practices, which, in turn, help the construction of common knowledge at the boundaries of the areas of specialty. Such common practices help reduce, or even eliminate, the negative effects of culture and the cultural differences, thus contributing to the success of the KM, whatever the approach adopted to manage the knowledge boundaries. Note that these common practices arising from a culture favoring KM can be considered to be boundary objects. Generally speaking, organizational culture is one of the instruments necessary for the success of the KM approaches proposed by Carlile [CAR 04]. The case of NSN's culture is an illustration of this observation.

Through the analysis succinctly presented in this section, we have seen the complementarity between the research model employed here – "design of the learning organization" – and the framework put forward by Carlile [CAR 04] to manage knowledge boundaries. Indeed, the new model used here supplements the approaches advanced by this author, by identifying the conditions and the means necessary for their effective implementation.

Conclusion

In the foregoing chapters, we have presented both our empirical analyses and our theoretical propositions. We have integrated the determining factors for a knowledge management (KM) policy, cited in the literature, across the five dimensions of organizational design drawn from Galbraith's "star model" [GAL 73, GAL 02b] – namely strategy, incentive systems, people, technology (KMS) and structure.

Our analysis of KM in three contrasting organizational situations (before, during and after a merger) in regard to the same project teams exercising the same professional activities (bid preparation and solution development) has yielded results that are both convergent with and divergent from those described in the existing literature. Certain conditions for effective KM demonstrated in the literature were confirmed, others countered, some were absent and new conditions have emerged from the field.

In this regard, the main lessons which can be drawn from our theoretical and empirical study are as follows:

– In order to be implemented effectively, KM must constitute a strategic objective for the organization, supported by concrete initiatives on the part of the directors and the upper echelons of the hierarchy. This is a result shared by previous literature in the field and the study presented here.

– A policy of sustained, monitored and evaluated training is a crucially important factor for the successful implementation of a KM program. This condition confirms the results found by previous studies.

– Lack of trust in the management did not represent an obstacle to the development of KM during the SCCC phase (before the merger), in spite of the unfavorable position of numerous department heads and difficult financial conditions. Indeed, SCCC's employees never hesitated to share their knowledge and to support their colleagues, recognizing that the latter were not to blame for the management's unfair behavior. However, contrary to the conclusions advanced by Renzl [REN 08], our study detected that the lack of trust in the management during the period of the merger and the creation of the new company, NSN, strongly (though indirectly) weighed in favor of KM. Indeed, the lack of trust in the management during the merger was due to the management's lack of communication about the restructuring of the company and the impact it would have on the employees. Thus, the uncertainty as to the teams' future which was characteristic of this period seems to have encouraged the employees to share their experience and knowledge, both within their own team and between different teams. Perhaps, this is evidence of an inverse effect – that is to say that the uncertainty about the future in which the teams were kept by the management actually encouraged them to share their experiences more freely. Hence, mutual assistance, solidarity and trust between colleagues constitute a decisive factor in the development of knowledge.

– Individual characteristics such as age and gender, hierarchical level and previous experience of exchange, cited in the preexisting literature, do not appear to have a significant impact on the implementation of a KM program and the use of KMSs, but this may be due to the uniformity of the sample examined in this study. Only language, prior experience and national culture had a notable effect on the individuals' behavior in terms of managing their knowledge.

– The characteristics of ease of use and perceived usefulness of the KMSs need to be taken into account. The study also shows that incentives to the use of KMSs and improvement of the quality of those tools are factors which are favorable to the spread of their use.

– Finally, regarding the structural conditions, our results bear out the findings of other research into the correlation between the number of hierarchical levels and the success of KM. In this regard, it was noted that a large number of hierarchical levels increases employees' reticence to share their knowledge; thus, this factor constitutes an obstacle to effective KM.

With our research as it currently stands, we can state that, when the merger reached a sufficient level of maturity, there was no longer any discontinuity in knowledge sharing within NSN. Quite the opposite, in fact, there was a significant rise in KM activities in the company, encouraged by NSN's corporate culture, through the use of KMSs and face-to-face contact, often supported by the use of remote communication and mobile phone technology (SMS), facilitating the transfer of both explicit and tacit knowledge. The use of these technologies is a novelty associated with the culture of the company N, introduced after the merger. On this point, our case study of a merger differs from the one conducted by Yoo et al. [YOO 07].

We also noted, following the analysis of the results from the three phases, that:

– during the first phase of the study, KM in the company was weak, due to multiple instances of failure – organizational, technical and cultural;

– next, during the second phase (the period of the merger), characterized by the introduction of the culture of the partner company, N, and by an organizational context of instability, uncertainty and little security, the employees and the management both worked to create a new dynamic, which impelled and (sometimes inadvertently) revitalized KM in the newly formed company, NSN;

– finally, when the merger had reached a certain level of maturity and a more stable environment had been established, we noted that certain conditions of the development of KM became variable, contradictory or ambivalent. This ambivalence is due to the threefold effect of culture (national culture, organizational culture, and professional culture).

Not only do these three cultural profiles influence the process of KM, but in turn, the practices of KM adopted may also contribute to the construction of a professional culture and consolidation of an organizational culture which can absorb all the cultural differences (national culture) that cause the variability of the behaviors associated with KM in the organization. Thus, we can conclude that culture and KM exert reciprocal influences on one another.

The links between culture and KM can also be analyzed in terms of knowledge boundaries and boundary objects used to manage those boundaries. Indeed, to varying degrees, all three cultural profiles contribute to the creation of knowledge boundaries. Such is the case, notably, with national culture which gives rise to differences between the organizational actors and, therefore, between their behaviors in relation to KM. In parallel, the professional and organizational cultures emerging from the KM practices within the organization often contribute significantly to the creation of boundary objects facilitating knowledge sharing by the creation of shared knowledge. That knowledge, shared by the members of a project team, in turn helps to adjust and consolidate the organizational and professional cultures.

Outcome of the study

Theoretical contributions

The model presented in this book – the design of the learning organization, which is different to Galbraith's star model [GAL 73, GAL 02b] – aimed to analyze and understand the development of the process of KM in a rich organizational environment. The benefits of KM are well recognized, both for corporations and for research institutes. Thus, managers and researchers are constantly on the lookout for means, methods, technologies and solutions that help to efficiently manage the knowledge resource. The deployment of our model in three contrasting organizational situations (before, during and after the merger) helped to enrich the results already known from the existing literature and to enrich our own model.

One of the other contributions made by this research lies in the mobilization and articulation of several distinct theoretical fields around the domain of KM in order to better explain how the knowledge resource develops in project teams. The research draws on the seminal works in KM and works on the management of information systems.

In addition, the triple effect of culture (national, organizational and professional) on the development of the KM process constitutes a new observation in the domain of KM, which warrants further investigation in light of the works on the links between KM in organizations and the different cultures which characterize those organizations.

Finally, we feel that the use of work on organizational design, cultures and management of knowledge boundaries also constitutes a contribution to research on KM.

Managerial contributions of the study

In parallel to the theoretical and methodological contributions, a work of research in management science and information systems must have practical contributions. There are multiple managerial advantages to our research. The study gives companies the possibility to diagnose the conditions for development of effective KM and, thus, to identify the means of action to favor knowledge sharing and learning, whether via KMSs or by face-to-face relations.

In addition, KM does and always will constitute a topical theme both for academics and for managers. The study of the state of KM during three different phases (before the merger, during the period when the new structure was being established and in a period of stability and maturity of the new structure) will enable directors to take an objective view of these three phases and to observe the evolutions and changes linked to this domain in three different contexts. In addition, KM, its processes and its tools have provided an effective way to ensure the mixing and integration of two different communities (company S and company N), thus leading to a new community: company NSN. Thus, the empirical analyses in this study can offer the managers additional illumination with which to examine the establishment of a KM program in the context of a merger.

Having conducted this research, we can provide managers with a list of organizational factors that they must take into account in order to create a context propitious to the development of effective KM within their teams.

The study's contributions for the researcher

One of the contributions of this research results from our total immersion over 12 months in the world of business, which can provide a reading on the richness of the data and the accuracy of the results. In addition, this experience allows us to measure our "social usefulness" against two distinct referential frameworks. The first is an academic frame of reference, wherein "usefulness" is measured in relation to the value of the lessons delivered and to the academic quality of the publications and other research. The second is a non-academic referential framework, where "usefulness" is measured in relation to the relevance of the lessons delivered and research carried out for the world of business or more generally for the life of organizations. It is incumbent upon every lecturing researcher in the area of management to find his/her own balance between these two frames of reference [THI 03].

One of the most important contributions made by this study is the originality of the field of study. This originality results from the occurrence of an important event – in this case, that of the merger between the two companies N and S – at the moment when we were in the field, conducting our empirical study, whose results reflect the changes and transformations caused by such an event. Often, researchers are present in the field at moments of stability for the companies they study and rarely in periods of upheaval. Thus, we had the rare opportunity to collect data before that event and, hence, were able to be present and observe the KM practices in two different structures, and the evolution of those practices, because of the cross-cutting nature of the study.

The limitations of the study

This study enabled us to answer the questions linked to the issue at hand in this book. However, like any theoretical and empirical research, it does have certain inevitable limits. The first limitation pertains to the difficulties encountered in the field and the difficulty for us to integrate ourselves into the company and be accepted by all the employees. These difficulties, which were encountered at the start of the study and over the course of the first few months, are due to the company being unused to playing host to a researcher from an academic environment but also due to the researcher in question belonging to a research center located in France: a country that is outside of the company's theater of activity. Thus, it was difficult for us to gain acceptance, as an outsider coming both from a different domain of activity and from another country outside the region to which the competence center constituting the field of this study belongs. In addition to these difficulties experienced by us in the field as an external actor, there were other difficulties linked to the efforts made: first, to convince the hierarchical leaders of the study's usefulness and, second, to integrate into the company.

Furthermore, being present in the field at the moment of a new event affecting the company can represent both an opportunity and a constraint for a researcher, resulting from the instability of the working environment, which can lead to difficulties in data collection, interpretation of the results and their generalization to apply more broadly.

In a field study, it is not possible to collect data about every single aspect of the organization; thus, choices need to be made in order to determine the scope of the data harvesting. The sample for the study at hand was composed solely of people of Tunisian nationality, belonging to the old company, S. Hence, expatriates belonging to S and the employees of N were excluded from the pool. Thus, this analysis is limited to the point of view of only one of the stakeholders in the merger. In this research, it has not been possible either to carry out other case studies for comparative purposes or conduct a quantitative study for the purpose of triangulation of the data. However, this is something the researcher wishes to envisage for the future, in order to extend the validity of the results, both internally and externally.

Indeed, the choice was made to carry out only one empirical study within a single organization, which has certain specific characteristics. This choice could influence the validity of the results obtained. It would be ideal, if possible, to try to increase the number of cases examined and, thus, carry out other case studies in different environments. Nonetheless, this case study enabled us to look at very varied empirical material, which is one of the strengths of the study.

Finally, note that the use of qualitative methods also brings with it certain limitations. Although those limitations do not jeopardize the validity of the results obtained, it is worth briefly discussing them, in order to better be able to circumvent them in future research. They pertain to the choice to carry out a qualitative study, in that qualitative research has often been criticized for lack of objectivity, validity or academic rigor. The main source of these criticisms has been the school of thought favoring a quantitative approach to research, which holds that reality is objective and measurable. When a qualitative study is properly carried out, it is entirely pertinent, shedding particular light on complex social phenomena. In that sense, the criticism leveled at qualitative research can be ignored in this particular case.

Having admitted these limitations, it now makes sense to suggest some possible future research directions, which could contribute to the progress of KM.

Prospective research directions

There are many viable research directions that could be pursued in light of the current work.

To begin with, the researcher could try to achieve greater depth of analysis using data collected during the case study, which have only been partially exploited for this publication.

A second research direction is to try to enrich these analyses by conducting new empirical investigations:

– first, in that same context of project teams, by attempting to redirect our focus along other possible paths, interviewing the line managers rather than the ordinary members of the project teams or expanding the field of investigation to the MEA region, by studying several countries in that region in order to compare the results;

– next, by planning a future return to the field to conduct a complementary quantitative study, interviewing the line managers in NSN – in the MEA region, inspired by a work of research similar to this one: that of Hansen [HAN 07], taking account of the variables of performance of KM;

– finally, the results obtained in this study could be compared to the conclusions set out in other contexts, other domains of activity – notably other cases of KM in a situation of a corporate merger, such as the cases studied by Grotenhuis and Weggeman [GRO 02], Carrillo and Anumba [CAR 02b] and Yoo et al. [YOO 07].

These research prospects ought to contribute to improving the understanding of the conditions of development of effective KM in a project team and, by supplementing the research presented in this book, help to produce theories specific to the schools of KM and information systems.

Bibliography

[ADA 92] ADAMS D., NELSON R., TODD P., "Perceived usefulness, ease of use, and usage of information technology: a replication", *MIS Quarterly*, vol. 16, no. 2, June, pp. 227–247, 1992.

[AFI 92] AFITEP-AFNOR, *Vocabulaire de gestion de projet*, 2nd ed. Editions Afnor, Paris, 1992.

[ALA 00] ALAVI M., "Managing organizational knowledge", in ZMUD R. (ed.), *Framing the Domains of IT Management: Projecting the Future through the Past*, Pinnaflex, New York, 2000.

[ALA 01] ALAVI M., LEIDNER D., "Knowledge management and knowledge management systems: conceptual foundations and research issues", *MIS Quarterly*, vol. 25, no. 1, pp. 107–176, 2001.

[ANA 11] ANAND A., SINGH M. "Understanding Knowledge Management: A Literature Review", *International Journal of Engineering Science and Technology*, vol. 3, no. 2, pp. 926–939, 2011.

[AND 05] ANDREANI J.C., CONCHON F., "Méthodes d'analyse et d'interprétation des études qualitatives: état de l'art en marketing", *Proceedings of the 4th International Marketing Trends Conference*, Paris, 2005.

[ARD 06] ARDICHVILI A., MAUER M., LI W. *et al.*, "Cultural influences on knowledge sharing through online communities of practice", *Journal of Knowledge Management*, vol. 10, no. 1, pp. 94–107, 2006.

[ARG 90] ARGOTE L., BECKMAN S.L., EPPLE D., "The persistence and transfer of learning in industrial settings", *Management Science*, vol. 36, pp. 140–154, 1990.

[ARG 00] ARGOTE L., INGRAM P., LEVINE J.M., *et al.*, "Knowledge transfer in organizations: learning from the experience of the others", *Organizational Behavior and Human Decision Processes*, vol. 82, no. 1, pp. 1–8, 2000.

[ARG 64] ARGYRIS C., *Integrating the Individual and the Organization*, Wiley & Sons, New York, 1964.

[ARG 95] ARGYRIS C., *Savoir pour Agir, Surmonter les obstacles de l'Apprentissage Organisationnel*, InterEditions, Paris, 1995.

[ARG 78] ARGYRIS C., SCHÖN D.A., *Organizational Learning: A Theory of Action Perspective*, Addison-Wesley, Reading, MA, 1978.

[ARG 02] ARGYRIS C., SCHÖN D.A., *Apprentissage organisationnel, théorie, méthode, pratique*, De Boeck University, Brussels, 2002.

[AVE 89] AVENIER M.J., "Méthodes recherche de terrain et recherche en management stratégique", *Economies et Sociétés, série sciences de gestion*, no. 14, pp. 199–218, 1989.

[BAN 03] BANSLER J., HAVN E., "Building community knowledge systems: an empirical study of IT-support for sharing best practices among managers", *Knowledge and Process Management*, vol. 10, no. 3, pp. 156–163, 2003.

[BAI 02a] BAILE S., LANCINI A., "Les déterminants de l'adoption d'un système de gestion des connaissances", *Actes de la 11ème conférence de l'AIMS*, 2002.

[BAI 02c] BAILLETTE B., LEBRATY J.F., "De la gestion des relations dans l'équipe virtuelle : la place de la confiance", *Actes du 7ème Colloque de l'AIM*, Tunisia, Hammamet, 30 May–1 June, 2002.

[BAI 02b] BAILLETTE P., LEBRATY J.F., "L'utilisation des systèmes d'aide à la décision de groupe : une approche en termes d'apprentissage et de gestion des relations", in ROWE F., *Faire de la Recherche en Système d'Information*, Editions Vuibert, Paris, 2002.

[BAR 09] BARACHINI F., "Cultural and social issues for knowledge sharing", *Journal of Knowledge Management*, vol. 13, no. 1, pp. 98–110, 2009.

[BAR 77] BARDIN L., *L'Analyse de Contenu*, Presses Universitaires de France, Paris, 1977.

[BAR 04] BAREIL C., Préoccupations, appropriation et efficacité des membres et des animateurs des communautés virtuelles: la dimension individuelle – Gestion du changement, CEFRIO, Quebec, Collection Recherche et Etudes de Cas, 2004.

[BAR 06] BAREL Y. "Fusions – acquisitions internationales: le choc des cultures", *La Revue des Sciences de Gestion, Direction et Gestion*, no. 218, March-April, pp. 53–60, 2006.

[BAR 86] BARNEY J.B., "Strategic factor markets: Exceptions, luck and business strategy", *Management Science*, vol. 32, pp. 1231–1241, 1986.

[BAR 91] BARNEY J.B., "Firm, resources and sustained competitive advantage", *Journal of Management*, vol. 1, pp. 99–120, 1991.

[BAR 04] BARRETT M., CAPPLEMAN S., SHOIB G., *et al.*, "Learning in knowledge communities: managing technology and context", *European Management Journal*, vol. 22, no. 1, February, pp. 1–11, 2004.

[BAR 02] BARZANTNY C. "L'entreprise et l'internationalisation: les clés de la réussite d'un projet international", *Personnel-ANDCP*, no. 433, pp. 13–17, 2002.

[BAT 84] BATE P., "The impact of organizational culture on approaches to organizational problem – solving", *Organization Studies*, vol. 5, no. 1, pp. 43–66, 1984.

[BAT 08] BATESON G., *Vers une écologie de l'esprit, Vol. 2*, Editions du Seuil, Paris, 2008.

[BAU 99] BAUMARD P., DONADA C., IBERT J., XUEREB J.-M., "La collecte des données et la gestion de leurs sources", in THIÉTART R.A. (coord.), *Méthodes de recherche en management*, Editions Dunod, Paris, 1999.

[BEC 08] BECERRA M., LUNNAN R., HUEMER L., "Trustworthiness, risk, and the transfer of tacit and explicit knowledge between alliance partners", *Journal of Management Studies*, vol. 45, no. 4, pp. 691–713, 2008.

[BEC 10] BECERRA-FERNANDEZ I., SABHERWAL R., *Knowledge Management: Systems and Processes*, M.E. Sharpe, New York, 2010.

[BEL 94] BÉLANGER L., *Culture organisationnelle – Bibliographie analytique et thématique (1980–1992)*, Les Presses de l'Université Laval, Laval, Québec, 1994.

[BEN 07] BEN CHOUIKHA M., "Les communautés de pratiques entre le travail à distance et le présentiel: Cas des Clubs VINCI Energies", *Actes du Colloque AIM'2007*, HEC Lausanne, Suisse, 2007.

[BEN 08] BEN CHOUIKHA M., DAKHLI S., "The knowledge-gap reduction in software engineering", *Proceedings of the 2nd Mediterranean Conference on Information Systems (MCIS'2008)*, Hammamet, Tunisia, 2008.

[BEN 09a] BEN CHOUIKHA M., MARCINIAK R., "Management de connaissances en situation de fusion", *Actes du colloque AIM'2009*, Marrakech, Morocco, 2009.

[BEN 09b] BEN CHOUIKHA M., DAKHLI S., "A multi-view model of knowledge management", *Proceedings of the SIIE'2009 Conference*, Hammamet, Tunisia, 2009.

[BEN 10a] BEN CHOUIKHA M., Design de l'organisation apprenante: une étude longitudinale des équipes projet 'Nokia Siemens Networks Communication Competences Center', PhD Thesis, Paris-Dauphine University, 2010.

[BEN 11] BEN CHOUIKHA M., DAKHLI S., "Knowledge sharing enablers and barriers: the case of virtual organizations", *Proceedings of the 5th Mediterranean Conference on Information Systems (MCIS'2011)*, Limassol, Cyprus, 2011.

[BEN 12] BEN CHOUIKHA M., DAKHLI S., "The dimensions of knowledge sharing", *Proceedings of the 6th Mediterranean Conference on Information Systems (MCIS'2012)*, Guimarães, Portugal, 2012.

[BEN 15a] BEN CHOUIKHA M., DAKHLI S., "Un cadre théorique pour l'analyse des multiples facettes des systèmes de management des connaissances", *Actes du colloque AIM'2015*, Rabat, Morocco, 2015.

[BEN 15b] BEN CHOUIKHA M., DAKHLI S., "Knowledge sharing in computerization projects: an approach based on boundary objects", *Proceedings of the 9th Mediterranean Conference on Information Systems (MCIS'2015)*, Samos, Greece, 2015.

[BEN 14] BENCSIK A., "Why do not knowledge management systems operate?", *Problems of Management in the 21st Century*, vol. 9, no. 1, pp. 18–26, 2014.

[BER 52] BERELSON B., *Content Analysis in Communication Research*, The Free Press, 1952.

[BER 03] BERG B., *Qualitative Research Methods for the Social Sciences*, 5th ed., Allyn and Bacon, Boston, MA, 2003.

[BER 68] BERTALANFFY, VON L., *General System Theory*, Braziler, New York, 1968.

[BER 93] BERTALANFFY VON L., *Théorie générale des systèmes*, Editions Dunod, Paris, 1993.

[BEY 03] BEYOU C., *Manager les connaissances: du knowledge management au développement des compétences dans l'organisation*, Liaisons, Paris, 2003.

[BHA 02] BHAGAT R., KEDIA B., TRIANDIS H., "Cultural variation in the cross-border transfer of organizational knowledge: an integrative framework", *Academy of Management Review*, vol. 27, no. 2, pp. 204–221, 2002.

[BLI 99] BLIN J.-F., *Représentations, pratiques et identités professionnelles*, L'Harmattan, Paris, 1999.

[BOC 05] BOCK G.W., ZMUD R.W., KIM Y.G. *et al.*, "Behavioral intention formation in knowledge sharing: examining the roles of extrinsic motivators, social-psychological forces and organizational climate", *MIS Quarterly*, vol. 29, no. 1, pp. 37–111, 2005.

[BOH 94] BOHN R.E., "Measuring and managing technological knowledge", *Sloan Management Review*, vol. 36, no. 1, pp. 14–21, 1994.

[BON 85] BONOMA T.V., "Case research in marketing: opportunities, problems, and a process", *Journal of Marketing Research*, vol. 22, pp. 199–208, 1985.

[BOU 56] BOULDING K.E., *The Image: Knowledge in Life and Society*, University of Michigan Press, Ann Arbor, MI, 1956.

[BOU 85] BOULDING K.E., *The World as a Total System*, Sage Publications, London, 1985.

[BOU 00] BOUNFOUR A., "Gestion des connaissances et systèmes d'incitation: entre théorie du 'Hau' et théorie du 'Ba'", *Systèmes d'Information et Management*, vol. 5, no. 2, pp. 7–40, 2000.

[BOU 03] BOUNFOUR A., "Gestion de la connaissance et devenir(s) des organisations", *Systèmes d'Information et Management*, vol. 8, no. 3, pp. 3–10, 2003.

[BOU 04a] BOURDON I., Les facteurs de succès des systèmes intégratifs d'aide à la gestion des connaissances, PhD Thesis, University of Montpellier II, 2004.

[BOU 04b] BOURHIS A., TREMBLAY D.D., Les facteurs organisationnels de succès des communautés de pratiques virtuelles, CEFRIO, Collection Recherche et Etudes de Cas, Quebec, 2004.

[BRO 91] BROWN J.S., DUGUID P., "Organization learning and communities of practices: toward a unified view of learning and innovation", *Organisation Organization Science*, vol. 2, no. 1, pp. 40–57, 1991.

[BRO 98] BROWN J.S., DUGUID P., "Organizing knowledge", *California Management Review*, vol. 40, no. 3, pp. 90–111, 1998.

[BUC 92] BUCHER R., STRAUSS A., "Professions in process", *American Journal of Sociology*, vol. 66, no. 4, 1961.

[CAB 90] CABIN P., "Compétences et organisation", in *Les Organisations*, Editions Sciences Humaines, Paris, 1999.

[CAL 91] CALORI R., SARNIN P., "Corporate culture and economic performance: a French study", *Organization Studies*, vol. 12, no. 1, pp. 49–74, 1991.

[CAR 02a] CARLILE P.R., "A pragmatic view of knowledge and boundaries: boundary objects in new product development", *Organization Science*, vol. 13, no. 4, pp. 442–455, 2002.

[CAR 04] CARLILE P.R., "Transferring, translating, and transforming: an integrative framework for managing knowledge across boundaries", *Organization Science*, vol. 15, no. 5, pp. 555–568, 2004.

[CAR 05] CARLILE P.R., ØSTERLUND C., "Relations in practice: sorting through practice theories on knowledge sharing in complex organizations", *Information Society*, vol. 21, pp. 91–107, 2005.

[CAR 03] CARLILE P.R., REBENTISCH E.S., "Into the black box: the knowledge transformation cycle", *Management Science*, vol. 49, no. 9, pp. 1180–1195, 2003.

[CAR 02b] CARRILLO P., ANUMBA C., "Knowledge management in the AEC sector: an exploration of the mergers and acquisitions context", *Knowledge and Process Management*, vol. 9, no. 3, pp. 49–161, 2002.

[CAZ 00] CAZAL D., "Culturalisme, comparaisons internationales et GRH: une analyse en terme de réflexivité", *Revue de Gestion des Ressources Humaines*, no. 37, pp. 6–23, 2000.

[CEF 05] CEFRIO, Travailler, apprendre et collaborer en réseau available at: www.cefrio. qc.ca/media/uploader/travailler_apprendre_collaborer.pdf, 2005.

[CHA 00a] CHANAL V., "Communautés de pratique et management par projet: à propos de l'ouvrage de Wenger" *Communities of Practice: Learning Meaning and Identity*, *M@n@gement*, vol. 3, no. 1, pp. 1–30, 2000.

[CHA 90] CHANLAT, J-F., *L'individu dans l'organisation. Les dimensions oubliées*, Les Presses de l'Université de Laval, Editions Eska, 1990.

[CHA 03] CHARBIT C., FERNANDEZ V., Sous le régime des communautés: Interactions cognitives et collectifs en ligne, Working paper, September, Ecole Nationale des Télécommunications de Paris, Paris, 2003.

[CHA 95] CHARREIRE-PETIT S., L'apprentissage organisationnel, proposition d'un modèle. Le cas d'une innovation managériale, PhD Thesis, Paris-Dauphine University, 1995.

[CHA 00b] CHAUVEL D., DESPRES C. eds, *Knowledge Horizons: The Present and the Promise of Knowledge Management*, Butterworth-Heinemann, Boston, MA, 2000.

[CHE 81] CHECKLAND P., *Systems Thinking, Systems Practice*, John Wiley & Sons, London, 1981.

[CHE 90] CHECKLAND P., *Soft Systems Methodology in Action*, John Wiley & Sons, London, 1990.

[CHE 98] CHEN C., CHEN X., MENDL J., "How can cooperation be fostered? The cultural effect of individualism-collectivism", *Academy of Management Review*, vol. 23, no. 2, pp. 285–304, 1998.

[CHI 01] CHIASSON M.W., LOVATO C.Y., "Factors influencing the formation of a user's perceptions and use of a DSS software Innovation", *The Data Base for Advances in Information Systems*, vol. 32, no. 3, pp. 16–35, 2001.

[CHI 07] CHIN-LOY C., MUJTABA B., "The influence of organizational culture on the success of knowledge management practices with North American companies", *International Business & Economics Research Journal*, vol. 6, no. 3, pp. 15–28, 2007.

[CHM 12] CHMIELECKI M., "Cultural barriers of knowledge management – a case of Poland", *Journal of Intercultural Management*, vol. 4, no. 2, pp. 100–110, 2012.

[CHO 94] CHOW C.W., KATO Y., SHIELDS M.D., "National culture and the preference for management controls: an exploratory study of the firm-labor market interface", *Accounting, Organization and Society*, vol. 19, no. 4-5, pp. 381–400, 1994.

[CLA 96] CLARK T., STODDARD D., "Inter-organizational business process redesigning: merging technological and process innnovation", *Journal of Management Information Systems*, vol. 13, no. 2, pp. 9–28, 1996.

[COH 97] COHEN S., BAILEY D.E., "What makes teams work: group effectiveness research from the shop floor to the executives suite", *Journal of Management*, vol. 23, no. 3, pp. 239–290, 1997.

[COH 90] COHEN W., LEVINTHAL D., "Absorptive capacity: A new perspective on learning and innovation", *Administrative Science Quaterly*, vol. 35, no. 3, pp. 128–152, 1990.

[CON 00] CONNELLY C., KELLOWAY K., Predictors of knowledge sharing in organizations, MSc Thesis, Queen's University, Kingston, Canada, 2000.

[CON 96] CONNER K., PRAHALAD C.K., "A resource-based theory on the firms: knowledge versus opportunism", *Organization Science*, vol. 7, no. 5, pp. 477–499, 1996.

[CON 94] CONSTANT D., KIESLER S., SPROUL L., "What's mine in ours, or is it? A study of attitudes about information sharing", *Information Systems Research*, vol. 5, no. 4, pp. 400–421, 1994.

[COO 01] COOKE N.J., KIEKEL P.A., HELM E.E., "Measuring team knowledge during skill acquisition of a complex task", *International Journal of Cognitive Ergonomics*, vol. 5, no. 3, pp. 297–315, 2001.

[COO 93] COOPER R.G., *Winning at New Products: Accelerating the Process from Idea to Launch*, Addison-Wesley, Reading, MA, 1993.

[COW 97] COWAN R., FORAY D., "The economics of codification and the diffusion of knowledge", *Industrial and Corporate Change*, vol. 6, no. 3, pp. 595–622, 1997.

[CRO 00] CROSS R., BAIRD L., "Technology is not enough: improving performance by building organization-al memory", *Sloan Management Review*, pp. 69–78, 2000.

[CYE 63] CYERT R.M., MARCH J.G., *The Behavioral Theory of the Firm*, Prentice-Hall, Englewood Cliffs, NJ, 1963.

[DAL 11] DALKIR K., *Knowledge Management in Theory and Practice*, 2nd ed., MIT Press, Cambridge, MA, 2011.

[DAL 75] DALY J.A., MILLER M.D., "The empirical development of an instrument to measure writing apprehension", *Research in the Teaching of English*, vol. 9, pp. 242–249, 1975.

[DAM 05] DAMERON S., JOSSERAND E., "Le processus de développement d'une communauté de pratique: une approche par la dialectique participation-réification", *Actes de la 14ème conférence de l'AIMS*, Angers, 2005.

[DAV 98a] DAVENPORT, T.H., PRUSAK L., *Working Knowledge: How Organizations Manage What They Know*, Harvard Business School Press, Boston, MA, 1998.

[DAV 98b] DAVENPORT T.H., DE LONG D.W., BEERS M., "Successful knowledge management projects", *Sloan Management Review*, vol. 39, no. 2, pp. 43–57, 1998.

[DAV 89] DAVIS F.D., "Perceived usefulness, perceived ease of use, and user acceptance of information technology", *MIS Quarterly*, vol. 13, no. 3, pp. 319–340, 1989.

[DAV 85] DAVIS M.H., OLSON J., AJENSTAT J.L., *et al.*, *Système d'information pour le management*, Editions Economica, Paris, 1985.

[DEM 06] DE MONTIGNY P., Analyse critique du discours de la culture organisationnelle, Thesis, HEC Montreal, 2006.

[DER 75] DE ROSNAY J., *Le Macroscope*, Editions du Seuil, Paris, 1975.

[DES 94] DESANCTIS G., POOLE M.S., "Capturing the complexity in advanced technology use: adaptive structuration theory", *Organization Science*, vol. 5, no. 2, pp. 121–147, 1994.

[DET 92] DE TERSSAC G., *Autonomie dans le travail*, Presses Universitaires de France, Paris, 1992.

[DET 96] DE TERSSAC G., "Savoirs, compétences, et travail", in BARBIER, J.-M., *Savoirs théoriques et savoirs d'action*, Presses Universitaires de France, Paris, 1996.

[DEF 02] DEFÉLIX C., "Gérer les compétences et manager les connaissances : dépasser les contenus pour gérer des processus et des acteurs", *Management & Conjoncture Sociale*, no. 616, pp. 65–66, 2002.

[DEJ 01] DEJOUX C., *Les compétences au cœur de l'entreprise*, Editions d'Organisation, Paris, 2001.

[DEL 01] DELOITTE RESEARCH, Collaborative Knowledge Networks. Driving Workforce Performance through Web-enabled Communities, Internal report, 2001.

[DEL 02] DELONG D.W., FAHEY L., "Diagnosing cultural barriers to knowledge management", *Academy of Management Executive*, vol. 14, no. 4, pp. 113–127, 2002.

[DEM 03] DEMERS C., "L'entretien", in GIORDANO Y. (ed.), *Conduire un projet de recherche: une perspective qualitative*, Editions EMS, Caen, 2003.

[DEN 94] DENZIN K., LINCOLN Y., *Handbook of Qualitative Research*, Sage Publications, London, 1994.

[DES 03] DESANCTIS G., FAYARD, A-L., ROACH M. *et al.*, "Learning in online forums", *European Management Journal*, vol. 21, no. 5, pp. 565–577, 2003.

[DES 96] DESCOLONGES M., *Qu'est-ce qu'un métier?*, Presses Universitaires de France, Paris, 1996.

[DET 04] DETIENNE K., DYER G., HOOPES C. *et al.*, "Toward a model of effective knowledge management and directions for future research: culture, leadership and CKOs", *Journal of Leadership and Organizational Studies*, vol. 10, no. 4, pp. 26–43, 2004.

[DIE 00] DIENG R., CORBY O., GIRBOIN A. *et al.*, *Méthodes et outils pour la gestion des connaissances*, Editions Dunod, Paris, 2000.

[DIR 00] DIRKS K.T., "Trust in leadership and team performance: evidence from NCAA basketball", *Journal of Applied Psychology*, vol. 85, pp. 1004–1012, 2000.

[DIR 01] DIRKS K.T., FERRIN D.L., "The role of trust in organizational settings", *Organization Science*, vol. 12, pp. 450–467, 2001.

[DOD 93] DODGSON M., "Organizational learning: a review of some literatures", *Organization Studies*, vol. 14, no. 3, pp. 375–394, 1993.

[DUB 03] DUBAR C., TRIPIER P., *Sociologie des professions*, Armand Colin, Paris, 2003.

[DUB 04] DUBÉ L., Mieux comprendre le succès des communautés de pratique virtuelle par l'investigation des aspects technologiques, CEFRIO, Montreal, 2004.

[DUB 03] DUBÉ L., BOURHIS A., JACOB R., "The impact of structural characteristics on the launching of intentionally formed virtual communities of practice", *Cahiers du Gresi*, no. 03–09, Montréal, 2003.

[DWY 98] DWYER K.K., "Communication apprehension and learning style preferences: Correlations and implications for teaching", *Communication Education*, vol. 47, pp. 137–150, 1998.

[EDM 99] EDMONDSON A.C., "Psychological safety and learning behavior in work teams", *Administrative Science Quarterly*, vol. 44, pp. 350–383, 1999.

[EIS 89a] EISENHARDT K.M., "Building theories from case study research", *Academy of Management Review*, vol. 14, pp. 532–550, 1989.

[EIS 89b] EISENHARDT K.M., "Making fast strategic decisions in high velocity environments", *Academy of Management Journal*, vol. 32, no. 3, pp. 543–576, 1989.

[ERM 03] ERMINE J.L., *La gestion des connaissances*, Hermès-Lavoisier, Paris, 2003.

[ETO 91] ETOUNGA M.D., *L'Afrique a-t-elle besoin d'un programme d'ajustement culturel?*, Les Editions Nouvelles du Sud, Ivry-Sur-Seine, 1991.

[FAH 98] FAHEY L., PRUSAK L., "The eleven deadliest sins of knowledge management", *California Management Review*, vol. 40, no. 3, pp. 265–275, 1998.

[FIO 85] FIOL C.M., LYLES M., "Organizational Learning", *Academy of Management Review*, vol. 10, pp. 803–813, 1985.

[FUL 04] FULK J., HEINO R., FLANAGIN A.J., *et al.*, "A test of the individual action model for organizational information commons", *Organization Science*, vol. 15, no. 5, pp. 569–585, 2004.

[GAL 71] GALBRAITH J.R., "Matrix organization design: how to combine functional and project form", *Business Horizons*, February, pp. 29–40, 1971.

[GAL 73] GALBRAITH J.R., *Designing Complex Organizations*, Addison-Wesley Publishing Company, Reading, MA, 1973.

[GAL 77] GALBRAITH J.R., *Organization Design*, Addison-Wesley Publishing Company, Reading, MA, 1977.

[GAL 82] GALBRAITH J.R., "Designing the innovating organization", *Organizational Dynamics*, Winter, pp. 5–25, 1982.

[GAL 94] GALBRAITH J.R., *Competing with Flexible Lateral Organization*, Addison-Wesley Publishing Company, Reading, MA, 1994.

[GAL 00a] GALBRAITH J.R., *Designing the Global Corporation*, Jossy-Bass Publishers, San Francisco, CA, 2000.

[GAL 00b] GALBRAITH J.R., "The role of formal structure and process", in *Breaking the Code of Change*, Harvard Business School Press, Boston, MA, 2000.

[GAL 02a] GALBRAITH J.R., "Organizing to deliver solutions", *Organizational Dynamics*, vol. 31, no. 2, pp. 194–207, 2002.

[GAL 02b] GALBRAITH J.R., *Designing Organizations Executive Guide to Strategy Structure*, Jossy-Bass Publishers, San Francisco, CA, 2002.

[GAR 93] GARVIN D.A., "Building a learning organization", *Harvard Business Review*, vol. 71, no. 4, pp. 78–92, 1993.

[GIN 99] GINSBERG M., KAMBIL A., "Annotate: a web-based knowledge management support system for document collections", *Proceedings of the 32nd Hawaii International Conference on System Sciences*, IEEE Computer Society Press, 1999.

[GIO 03] GIORDANO Y., *Conduire un projet de recherchée. Une perspective qualitative*, Editions EMS, Paris, 2003.

[GIR 95] GIROD-SEVILLE M., "La mémoire organisationnelle", *Revue Française de Gestion*, no. 105, pp. 30–42, 1995.

[GLA 67] GLASER B., STRAUSS A., *The Discovery of Grounded Theory, Strategies for Qualitative Research*, Adline Publishing Company, Chicago, IL, 1967.

[GOU 69] GOULD R.L., "Roles in sociological field work", in DENZIN N.K., *Sociological Methods*, Aldine Publishing Company, Chicago, IL, 1969.

[GON 01] GONGLA P., RIZZUTO C.R., "Evolving communities of practice: IBM Global services experience", *IBM Systems Journal*, vol. 40, no. 4, pp. 842–862, 2001.

[GOO 98] GOODMAN P.S., DARR E.D., "Computer-aided systems and communities: mechanisms for organizational learning in distributed environments", *MIS Quarterly*, vol. 22, no. 4, pp. 417–441, 1998.

[GOU 04] GOURY M.L., "Impact de la gestion des connaissances sur l'efficacité des communautés de pratiques", *Association Internationale de Management Stratégique (AIMS)*, Normandy, June, 2004.

[GRA 91] GRANT R.M., "The resources-based theory of the competitive advantage: implications for strategy formulation", *California Management Review*, vol. 33, pp. 114–135, 1991.

[GRA 96a] GRANT R.M., "Prospering in dynamically-competitive environment: Organizational capability as knowledge integration", *Organization Science*, vol. 4, pp. 375–387, 1996.

[GRA 96b] GRANT R.M., "Toward a knowledge-based theory of the firm", *Strategic Management Journal*, vol. 17, pp. 109–122, 1996.

[GRA 93] GRAWITZ, M., *Méthodes des sciences sociales*, 9th ed., Dalloz, Paris, 1993.

[GRO 03] GROLEAU C., "L'observation", in GIORDANO Y. (ed.), *Conduire un projet de recherche. Une perspective qualitative*, Éditions EMS, Paris, 2003.

[GRO 02] GROTENHUIS F.D.J., WEGGEMAN M.P., "Knowledge management in international mergers", *Knowledge and Process Management*, vol. 9, no. 2, pp. 83–89, 2002.

[GRU 04] GRUNDSTEIN M., "De la capitalisation des connaissances au management des connaissances dans l'entreprise", in BOUGHAZALA I., ERMINE J.-L., *Management des connaissances en entreprises*, Hermès-Lavoisier, Paris, 2004.

[GUR 99] GURTEEN D., "Creating a Knowledge Sharing Culture", *Knowledge Management Magazine*, vol. 2, no. 5, 1999.

[HAH 00] HAHN J., SUBRAMANI M.R., "A framework of knowledge management systems: issues and challenges for theory and practice", *Proceedings of the International Conference on Information Systems (ICIS'2000)*, Brisbane, Australia, 2000.

[HAM 98] HAMILTON D., "Traditions, performances and postures in applied qualitative research", in DENZIN N., LINCOLN Y., *The Landscape of Qualitative Research: Theories and Issues*, Sage Publications, London, 1998.

[HAM 97] HAMPDEN-TURNER C., TROMPENAARS F., "Response to Geert Hofstede", *International Journal of Intercultural Relations*, vol. 21, no. 1, pp. 149–159, 1997.

[HAN 99] HANSEN M.T., "The search-transfer problem: the role of weak ties in sharing knowledge across organization subunits", *Administrative Science Quarterly*, vol. 44, pp. 82–111, 1999.

[HAN 07] HANSEN M.T., HAAS M.R., "Different knowledge, different benefits: Toward a productivity perspective on knowledge sharing in organizations", *Strategic Management Journal*, vol. 27, no. 11, pp. 1133–1153, 2007.

[HAN 99] HANSEN M.T., NOHRIA N., TIERNEY T.. "What's your strategy for managing knowledge?", *Harvard Business Review*, vol. 77, no. 2, pp. 106–116, 1999.

[HIL 02] HILDRETH P.M., KIMBLEN C., "The duality of knowledge", *Information Research*, vol. 8, no. 1, pp. 1368–1613, 2002.

[HIN 03] HINDS P.J., PFEFFER J., "Why organizations don't know what they know: cognitive and motivational factors affecting the transfer of expertise", in ACKERMAN M., PIPEK V., WULF V., *Sharing Expertise: Beyond Knowledge Management*, The MIT Press, Boston, MA, 2003.

[HIR 95] HIRSCHHEIM R., KLEIN H., LYYTINEN K., *Information Systems Development and Data Modeling: Conceptual and Philosophical Foundations*, Cambridge University Press, Cambridge, UK, 1995.

[HLA 02] HLADY RISPAL M., *La méthode des cas: Application à la recherche en gestion*, Editions De Boeck University, Brussels, 2002.

[HOF 80] HOFSTEDE G., *Culture's Consequences: International Differences in Work-Related Values*, Sage Publications, Beverly-Hills, CA, 1980.

[HOF 90] HOFSTEDE G., NEUIJEN, B, OHAVY D.-D., "Measuring organizational cultures: A qualitative and quantitative study across twenty cases", *Administrative Science Quarterly*, vol. 35, pp. 286–316, 1990.

[HOL 00] HOLSAPPLE C.W., JOSHI K.D., "An investigation of factors that influence the management of knowledge in organizations", *Journal of Strategic Information Systems*, vol. 9, no. 2–3, September, pp. 235–261, 2000.

[HOL 10] HOLSTE J.S., FIELDS D., "Trust and tacit knowledge sharing and use", *Journal of Knowledge Management*, vol. 14, no. 1, pp. 128–140, 2010.

[HUB 98] HUBER G.P., "Synergies between organisational learning and creativity and innovation", *Creativity and Innovation Management*, vol. 7, no. 1, pp. 3–8, 1998.

[HUB 01] HUBER G.P., "Transfer of knowledge in knowledge management system: unexplored issues and suggested studies", *Proceedings of the 9th European Conference on Information Systems*, pp. 72–79, 2001.

[HUB 91] HUBER G.P., "Organizational learning: the contributing processes and the literature", *Organization Science*, vol. 2, pp. 88–115, 1991.

[HUN 81] HUNT J.W., "Applying American behavioral science: some cross-cultural problems", *Organizational Dynamics*, vol. 10, no. 1, pp. 55–63, 1981.

[HUS 12] HUSTED K., "Knowledge-sharing hostility and governance mechanisms: an empirical test", *Journal of Knowledge Management*, vol. 16, no. 5, pp. 754–773, 2012.

[IRI 89] D'IRIBARNE P., *La logique de l'honneur: gestion des entreprises et traditions nationales*, Editions du Seuil, Paris, 1989.

[IRI 00] D'IRIBARNE P., "Management et cultures politiques", *Revue Française de Gestion*, no. 128, pp. 70–75, 2000.

[IRI 98] D'IRIBARNE P., HENRY A., SEGAL J.-P., *et al.*, *Cultures et mondialisation. Gérer par-delà les frontières*, Editions du Seuil, Paris, 1998.

[JAN 03] JANZ B., PRASAMPHANICH P., "Understanding the antecedents of effective knowledge management: the importance of a knowledge-centered culture", *Decision Sciences*, vol. 34, no. 2, pp. 351–384, 2003.

[JAR 01] JARVENPAA S.L., STAPLES S.D., "Exploring perceptions of organizational ownership of information and expertise", *Journal of Management Information Systems*, vol. 18, no. 1, pp. 151–183, 2001.

[JAR 00] JARVENPAA S.L., STAPLES D.S., "The use of collaborative electronic media for information sharing: an exploratory study of determinants", *Journal of Strategic Information Systems*, vol. 9, no. 2-3, pp. 129–154, 2000.

[JEN 00] JENNEX M.E., OLFMAN L., "Development recommendations for knowledge management/organizational memory systems", *Proceedings of the Information Systems Development Conference*, 2000.

[JEN 02] JENNEX M.E., OLFMAN L., "Organizational memory/knowledge effects on productivity, a longitudinal study", *Proceedings of the 35th Hawaii International Conference on System Sciences*, IEEE Computer Society, 2002.

[JEN 03] JENNEX M.E., OLFMAN L., ADDO T.B.A., "The need for an organizational knowledge management strategy", *Proceedings of the 36th Hawaii International Conference on System Sciences*, IEEE Computer Society, 2003.

[JIC 79] JICK T.D., "Mixing qualitative and quantitative methods: triangulation in action", *Administrative Science Quarterly*, vol. 24, no. 4, pp. 602–611, 1979.

[JON 11] JONES M., MUJTABA B., WILLIAMS A., *et al.*, "Organizational culture types and knowledge management in U.S. manufacturing firms", *Journal of Knowledge Management Practice*, vol. 72, no. 4, pp. 1–12, 2011.

[JOS 04] JOSSERAND E., "Les difficultés pratiques des communautés de pratiques", *Actes du 13ème congrès de l'AIMS*, 2004.

[JOS 02] JOSSERAND E., ISAAC H., "Structure et système d'information: quels rôles dans les pratiques de gestion de connaissances?", in KALIKA M. (ed.), *e-grh: Révolution ou évolution?*, Editions Liaisons, Paris, 2002.

[JUN 60] JUNKER B., *Field Work*, University of Chicargo Press, Chicago, IL, 1960.

[KAL 05] KALIKA M., BOUKEF N., ISAAC H., "La théorie du millefeuille : de la non substitution entre communication électronique et face-à-face", *Actes du 10ème congrès de l'AIM*, Toulouse, 2005.

[KAL 06] KALIKA M., *Management et TIC : 5 ans de e-management*, Editions Liaisons, Paris, 2006.

[KAL 07] KALIKA M., ISAAC H., BOUKEF N., "La théorie du millefeuille: de la non substitution entre communication électronique et face à face", *Revue Française de Gestion*, vol. 3, no. 172, pp. 117–129, 2007.

[KAN 05] KANHANHALI A., TAN B.C.Y., WEI K.K., "Contributing knowledge to electronic knowledge repositories: an empirical investigation", *MIS Quarterly*, vol. 29, no. 1, pp. 113–143, 2005.

[KAT 66] KATZ, D, KAHN R.L., *The Social Psychology of Organizations*, John Wiley & Sons, New York, 1996.

[KAT 74] KATZ R.L., "Skills of an effective administrator", *Harvard Business Review*, vol. 52, no. 5, pp. 90–102, 1974.

[KIN 06] KING W.R., "Knowledge sharing", in SCHWARTZ D. (ed.), *Encyclopedia of Knowledge*, Idea Group Publishing, Hershey, PA, 2006.

[KIN 07a] KING W.R., "IT strategy and innovation: recent innovation in knowledge management", *Information System Management*, vol. 24, pp. 91–93, 2007.

[KIN 07b] KING W.R., "A research agenda for the relationship between culture and knowledge management", *Knowledge and Process Management*, vol. 14, no. 3, pp. 226–236, 2007.

[KIN 01] KING W.R., KO D.-G., "Evaluating knowledge management and the learning organization: an information/knowledge value chain approach", *Communications of the Association for Information Systems*, vol. 5, 2001.

[KIN 08] KING W.R., MARKS P., "Motivating knowledge sharing through a knowledge management system", *Omega*, vol. 36, pp. 131–146, 2008.

[KOE 94] KOENIG R.M., THIETART R.A., "Contrôle limité et changement dans les organisations multidivisionnelles", *Actes de la 3ème Conférence Internationale de Management Stratégique*, Lyon, 9–11 May, 1994.

[KOG 92] KOGUT B., ZANDER U., "Knowledge of the firm, combinative capabilities and the replication of technology", *Organization Science*, vol. 3, no. 3, pp. 383–397, 1992.

[KOL 84] KOLB D.A., *Experiential Learning Experience as the Source of Learning and Development*, Prentice-Hall, Englewood Cliffs, NJ, 1984.

[KOS 01] KOSKINEN K.U., "Tacit knowledge as a promoter of success in technology firms", in *Proceedings of the 34th Hawaii International Conference on System Sciences*, IEEE Computer Society, 2001.

[KRI 03] KRIPPENDORFF K., *Content Analysis: An Introduction to Its Methodology*, 2nd ed., Sage Publications, Thousand Oaks, CA, 2003.

[KWO 09] KWONG K.K., LEVITT C.E., "The impact of national culture on value based decisions: Comparison of Saudi Arabian, Egyptian, and American healthcare professionals", *AHCMJ*, vol. 5, no. 2, pp. 79–91, 2009.

[LAN 01] LANCINI A., Les déterminants de l'adoption d'un système de gestion des connaissances: contribution à l'étude du succès de la technologie Lotus Notes dans une société mutuelle d'assurances, PhD Thesis, University of Toulouse I, 2001.

[LAN 03] LANCINI A., "Les déterminants du succès des Systèmes de Gestion des Connaissances (SGC): étude de cas d'une mutuelle d'assurances", *Actes du 8ème congrès de l'AIM*, Grenoble, June, 2003.

[LAN 04] LANG J.C., "Social context and social capital as enablers of knowledge integration", *Journal of Knowledge Management*, vol. 8, no. 3, pp. 89–105, 2004.

[LAV 91] LAVE J., WENGER E., *Situated Learning: Legitimate Peripheral Participation*, Cambridge University Press, New York, 1991.

[LAV 93] LAVE J., "The practice of learning", in CHAIKLIN S., LAVE J., *Understanding Practice: Perspectives on Activity and Context*, Cambridge University Press, Cambridge, 1993.

[LAW 67] LAWRENCE P., LORSCH J., "Differentiation and integration in complex organizations", *Administrative Science Quarterly*, vol. 12, no. 1, pp. 1–30, 1967.

[LEB 01] LE BOTERF G., *Compétences et navigation professionnelle*, Editions d'Organisation, Paris, 2001.

[LEB 02] LE BOTERF G., *Développer la compétence des professionnels, construire les parcours de professionnalisations*, Editions Liaisons, Paris, 2002.

[LEM 77] LE MOIGNE J.L., *La théorie du système général, Théorie de la modélisation*, Presses Universitaires de France, Paris, Collection Systèmes-Décisions, 1977.

[LEM 90] LE MOIGNE J.L., *La modélisation des systèmes complexes*, Editions Dunod, Paris, 1990.

[LEA 63] LEAVITT H.J., *The Social Science of Organizations, Four Perspectives*, Prentice-Hall, Englewood Cliffs, NJ, 1963.

[LEI 66] LEIBNIZ G.W., *Nouveaux essais sur l'entendement, humain*, Editions Garnier-Flammarion, Paris, 1966.

[LEO 98] LEONARD D., SENSIPER S., "The role of tacit knowledge in group innovation", *California Management Review*, vol. 40, no. 3, pp. 112–132, 1998.

[LES 00] LESSER E.L., FONTAINE M., SLUSHER J.A., *Knowledge and Communities*, Butterworth-Heinemann, Boston, MA, 2000.

[LEV 04] LEVIN D.Z., CROSS R., "The strength of weak ties you can trust: the mediating role of trust in effective knowledge transfer", *Management Science*, vol. 50, no. 11, pp. 1477–1490, 2004.

[LEV 00] LEVIN I., "Five windows into organization culture: an assessment framework and approach", *Organization Development Journal*, vol. 18, no. 1, pp. 83–94, 2000.

[LEV 88] LEVITT B., MARCH J., "Organizational learning", *Annual Review of Sociology*, vol. 14, pp. 319–340, 1988.

[LIM 97] LIMAYEM M., BERGERON F., RICHARD A., "Utilisation de la messagerie électroniques mesures objectives versus mesures subjectives", *Système d'Information et de Management*, vol. 2, no. 1, pp. 51–69, 1997.

[LOP 04] LOPEZ S.P., PEON J.M.M., ORDAS C.J.V., "Managing Knowledge: The Link Between Culture and Organizational Learning", *Journal of Knowledge Management*, vol. 8, no. 6, pp. 93–104.

[MAI 07] MAIER R., *Knowledge Management Systems: Information and Communication Technologies for Knowledge Management*, Springer-Verlag, Heidelberg, 2007.

[MAL 03] MALHOTRA Y., GALLETTA D.F., "Role of commitment and motivation in knowledge management systems implementation: theory, conceptualization, and measurement of antecedents of success", *Proceedings of the 36th Hawaii International Conference on System Sciences*, IEEE Computer Society Press, 2003.

[MAN 98] MANDVIWALLA M., EULGEM S., MOULD C., *et al.*, "Organizational memory systems design", Unpublished Working Paper for the *Task Force on Organizational Memory*, BURSTEIN F., HUBER G., MANDVIWALLA M., *et al.*, *Presented at the 31st Annual Hawaii International Conference on System Sciences*, 1998.

[MAR 91] MARCH J.G., "Exploration and exploitation in organizational learning", *Organization Science*, vol. 2, no. 1, pp. 71–87, 1991.

[MAR 75] MARCH J.G., OLSEN J.P., "The uncertainty of the past: organization learning under ambiguity", *European Journal of Political Research*, vol. 3, no. 2, pp. 147–171, 1975.

[MAR 58] MARCH J.G., SIMON H.A., *Organizations*, John Wiley & Sons, New York, 1958.

[MAR 99] MARCINIAK R., "Savoirs et apprentissage dans les organisations", *La Cible*, vol. 75, pp. 18–27, 1999.

[MAR 09] MARCINIAK R., ROWE F., *Systèmes d'Information, Dynamique et Organisation*, Editions Economica, Paris, 2009.

[MAR 01] MARKUS M.L., "Toward a theory of knowledge reuse: types of knowledge reuse situations and factors in reuse success", *Journal of Management Information Systems*, vol. 18, no. 1, pp. 57–93, 2001.

[MAR 88] MARKUS M.L., ROBEY D., "Information technology and organizational change, causal structure in theory and research", *Management Science*, vol. 34, no. 5, pp. 583–598, 1988.

[MAR 00] MARTENSSON M., "A critical review ok knowledge management as management tool", *Journal of Knowledge Management*, vol. 40, no. 4, pp. 204–216, 2000.

[MAY 95] MAYER R.C., DAVIS J.H., SCHOORMAN F.D., "An integrative model of organizational trust", *Academy of Management Review*, vol. 20, no. 3, pp. 709–734, 1995.

[MCC 04] MCCANN J.E., BUCKNER M., "Strategically integrating knowledge management initiatives", *Journal of Knowledge Management*, vol. 8, no. 1, pp. 47–63, 2004.

[MCD 00] MCDERMOTT R., "Community development as a natural step", *Knowledge Management Review*, vol. 3, no. 5, pp. 16–19, 2000.

[MCD 01] MCDERMOTT R., O'DELL C., "Overcoming cultural barriers to sharing knowledge", *Journal of Knowledge Management*, vol. 5, no. 1, pp. 76–85, 2001.

[MCD 99] MCDERMOTT R., "Why information technology inspired but cannot deliver knowledge management", *California Management Review*, vol. 41, no. 4, pp. 103–117.

[MCL 72] MC LUHAN M., *Pour comprendre les médias*, HMH, Montreal, 1972.

[MEL 72] MELEZE J., *L'analyse modulaire des systèmes de gestion*, Editions hommes et techniques A.M.S., Puteaux, 1972.

[MIL 94] MILES M.B., HUBERMAN A.M., *Qualitative Data Analysis: An Expanded Sourcebook*, 2nd ed., Sage Publications, London, 1994.

[MIL 03] MILES M.B., HUBERMAN A.M., *Analyse des données qualitatives*, 2nd ed., De Boeck University, Brussels, 2003.

[MIL 91] MILES M.B., HUBERMAN A.M., *Analyse des données qualitatives: Recueil de nouvelles méthodes*, De Boeck-Wesmael, Brussels, 1991.

[MIL 78] MILES R.E., SNOW C.C., *Organizational Strategy, Structure, and Process*, McGraw-Hill, New York, 1978.

[MIL 96] MILLER D., "A preliminary typology of organizational learning: synthesizing the literature", *Journal of Management*, vol. 22, no. 3, pp. 485–505, 1996.

[MIN 82] MINTZBERG H., *Structure et dynamique des organisations*, Editions d'Organisation, Paris, 1982.

[MON 08] MONNIER L., "L'influence des caractéristiques professionnelles sur la consultation d'un SGC et la capitalisation: le cas des métiers d'auditeur, d'avocat et de consultant", *Systèmes d'Information et Management*, vol. 13, no. 1, pp. 31–61, 2008.

[MOO 91] MOORE G.C., BENBASAT I., "Development of an instrument to measure the perceptions of adopting an information technology innovation", *Information Systems Research*, vol. 2, no. 3, pp. 192–222, 1991.

[MOR 77] MORIN E., *La méthode, tome 1: La nature de la nature*, Editions du Seuil, Paris, 1977.

[MUC 96] MUCCHIELLI A., *Dictionnaires des méthodes qualitatives en sciences humaines et sociales*, Armand Colin, Paris, 1996.

[MUL 02] MULLER M.J., CAREY K., "Design as a minority discipline in software company: toward requirements for a community of practice", *Proceedings of the CHI'2002 Conference*, Minneapolis, MN, 2002.

[MUR 14] AL MURAWWI M.A., BEHERY M., PAPANASTASSIOU M. *et al.*, "Examining the relationship between organizational culture and knowledge management: the moderation effect of organizational divisions at an Abu Dhabi Gas Company", *SAM Advanced Management Journal*, vol. 79, no. 2, pp. 48–59, 2014.

[NAY 08] NAYIR D., UZUN-CARSILI U., "A culture perspective on knowledge management: the success story of Sarkuysan Company", *Journal of Knowledge Management*, vol. 12, no. 2, pp. 141–155, 2008.

[NON 91] NONAKA I., "The knowledge creating company", *Harvard Business Review*, pp. 96–104, 1991.

[NON 94] NONAKA I., "A dynamic theory of organizational knowledge creation", *Organization Science*, vol. 5, no. 1, pp. 14–37, 1994.

[NON 95] NONAKA I., TAKEUCHI H., *The Knowledge Creating Company: How Japanese Companies Create the Dynamics of Innovation*, Oxford University Press, New York, 1995.

[OCD 96] OCDE, Rapport annuel de l'OCDE 1996, Paris, Publications de l'OCDE, 1996.

[OCD 00] OCDE, Rapport annuel de l'OCDE 2000, Paris, Publications de l'OCDE, 2000.

[ODE 98] O'DELL C., GRAYSON J., "If only we knew what we know: identification and transfer of internal best practices", *California Management Review*, vol. 40, no. 3, pp. 154–174, 1998.

[OKH 02] OKHUYSEN G.A., EISENHARDT K.M., "Integrating knowledge in groups: how formal interventions enable flexibility", *Organization Science*, vol. 13, no. 4, pp. 370–386, 2002.

[OLI 06] OLIVER S. KANDADI K.R., "How to develop knowledge culture in organizations? A multiple case study of large distributed organizations", *Journal of Knowledge Management*, vol. 10, no. 4, pp. 6–24, 2006.

[ONE 07] O'NEILL B., ADYA M., "Knowledge sharing and the psychological contract", *Journal of Managerial Psychology*, vol. 22, no. 4, pp. 411–436, 2007.

[ORD 04] ORDONEZ DE PABLOS P., "Knowledge flow transfers in multinational corporations: knowledge properties and implications for management", *Journal of Knowledge Management*, vol. 8, no. 6, pp. 105–116, 2004.

[ORL 92] ORLIKOWSKI W.J., "The duality of technology – rethinking the concept of technology in organizations", *Organization Science*, vol. 3, no. 3, pp. 398–427, 1992.

[ORL 00] ORLIKOWSKI W.J., "Using technology and constituting structures: a practice lens for studying technology in organizations", *Organization Science*, vol. 11, no. 4, pp. 404–428, 2000.

[ORL 91] ORLIKOWSKI W.J., BAROUDI J.J., "Studying information technology in organisations: research approaches and assumptions", *Information System Research*, vol. 2, no. 1, pp. 1–8, 1991.

[OST 02] OSTY F., *Le désir de Métier: engagement, identité et reconnaissance au travail*, Presses Universitaires de Rennes, Rennes, 2002.

[PAR 04] PARK H., RIBIERE V., SCHULTE W.D., "Critical attributes of organizational culture that promote knowledge management technology implementation success", *Journal of Knowledge Management*, vol. 8, no. 3, pp. 106–117, 2004.

[PAR 64] PARSONS T., *Social Structure and Personality*, Free Press, New York, 1964.

[PAU 04] PAUL D.L., MCDANIEL R.R., "A field study of the effect of interpersonal trust on virtual collaborative relationship performance", *MIS Quarterly*, vol. 28, no. 2, pp. 183–227, 2004.

[PEN 59] PENROSE E., *The Theory of the Growth of the firm*, Basil Blackwell, Oxford, 1959.

[PER 06] PERRIN A., "Le transfert inter-organisationnel des bonnes pratiques: quand l'entreprise joue au domino", *Actes de la XVème Conférence Internationale de Management Stratégique*, Geneva, June, 2006.

[PES 04] PESQUEUX Y., "Apprentissage organisationnel, économie de la connaissance: mode ou modèle", *Cahiers du LIPSOR*, no. 6, September, 2004.

[PES 06] PESQUEUX Y., FERRARY M., *Management de la connaissance*, Editions Economica, Paris, 2006.

[PET 79] PETTIGREW A.M., "On studying organizational cultures", *Administrative Science Quarterly*, vol. 24, no. 4, pp. 570–581, 1979.

[PIA 79] PIAGET J., *Epistémologie génétique*, Presses Universitaires de France, Paris, 1979.

[POL 67] POLANYI M., *The Tacit Dimension*, Doubleday, New York, 1967.

[PRA 97] PRAX J-Y., *Manager la connaissance dans l'entreprise: Les nouvelles technologies au service de l'ingénierie de la connaissance*, Editions INSEP, Paris, 1997.

[PRA 00] PRAX, J-Y. *Le Guide du Knowledge Management: Concepts et Pratiques de la Gestion des Connaissances*, Editions Dunod, Paris, 2000.

[PRA 07] PRAX, J-Y. *Le Manuel du Knowledge Management*, Editions Dunod, Paris, 2007.

[RAV 11] RAVISHANKAR M.N., PAN S.L., LEIDNER D.E., "Examining the strategic alignment and implementation success of a KMS: a subculture-based multilevel analysis", *Information Systems Research*, vol. 22, no. 1, pp. 39–59, 2011.

[REI 00] REIX R., *Systèmes d'information et management des organisations*, 3rd ed., Editions Vuibert, Paris, 2000.

[REI 04] REIX R., *Systèmes d'information et management des organisations*, 5th ed., Editions Vuibert, Paris, 2004.

[REN 08] RENZL B., "Trust in management and knowledge sharing: the mediating effects of fear and knowledge documentation", *Omega*, vol. 36, no. 2, pp. 206–220, 2008.

[RHE 93] RHEINGOLD H., *The Virtual Community: Homesteading on the Electronic Frontier*, Addison-Wesley, New York, 1993.

[RIE 05] RIEGE A., "Three-dozen knowledge-sharing barriers managers must consider", *Journal of Knowledge Management*, vol. 9, no. 3, pp. 18–35, 2005.

[ROB 00] ROBERTS J., "From know-how to show-how? Questioning the role of information and communication technologies in knowledge transfer", *Technology Analysis and Strategic Management*, vol. 12, no. 4, pp. 429–443, 2000.

[ROG 95] ROGERS E.M., *Diffusion of Innovations*, 4th ed., The Free Press, New York, 1995.

[ROL 00] ROLLAND N., CHAUVEL D., "Knowledge Transfer in Strategic Alliances", in DESPRES C., CHAUVEL D. (eds), *Knowledge Horizons*, Butterworth Heinemann, Boston, MA, 2000.

[ROS 07] ROSEN B., FURST S., BLACKBURN R., "Overcoming barriers to knowledge sharing in virtual teams", *Organizational Dynamics*, vol. 36, no. 3, pp. 259–273, 2007.

[ROY 99] ROYER I., ZARLOWSKI P., "Echantillon(s)", in THIETART R.-A., *Méthodes de recherché en Management*, Editions Dunod, Paris, 1999.

[RUB 01] RUBENSTEIN-MONTANO B., LIEBOWITZ J., BUCHWALTER J. *et al.*, "SMARTVision: a knowledge management method", *The Journal of Knowledge Management*, vol. 5, no. 4, pp. 300–310, 2001.

[RUG 98] RUGGLES R., "The state of the notion: knowledge management in practice", *California Management Review*, vol. 40, no. 3, pp. 80–89, 1998.

[SAC 07] SACKMANN A.S., FRIESL M., "Exploring cultural impacts on knowledge sharing behavior in project teams – results from a simulation study", *Journal of Knowledge Management*, vol. 11, no. 6, pp. 142–156, 2007.

[SAG 99] SAGE A.P., ROUSE W.B., "Information systems frontiers in knowledge management", *Information Systems Frontiers*, vol. 1, no. 3, pp. 205–219, 1999.

[SAI 01] SAINTY F., Mutuelles de santé et nouveaux contextes d'action: une approche par le modèle ressources-compétences, PhD Thesis, University of Nice Sophia-Antipolis, 2001.

[SAM 05] SAMBAMURTHY V., SUBRAMANI M., "Special issue on information technologies and knowledge management: special issue foreword", *MIS Quarterly*, vol. 29, no. 1, pp. 1–7, 2005.

[SAM 94] SAMBAMURTHY V., CHIN W.W., "The effects of group attitudes toward alternative GDSS designs on the decision-making performance of computer-supported groups", *Decision Sciences*, vol. 25, no. 2, pp. 215–242, 1994.

[SAM 95] SAMURÇAY R., PASTRE P., "La conceptualisation des situations de travail dans la formation des compétences. Le développement des compétences : analyse du travail et didactique professionnelle", *Education Permanente*, no. 123, pp. 13–32, 1995.

[SAU 31] SAUSSURE F., *Cours de Linguistique Générale*, Editions Payot, Paris, 1931.

[SCH 85] SCHEIN E.H., *Organizational Culture and Leadership*, 1st ed., Jossey-Bass, San Francisco, CA, 1985.

[SCH 92] SCHEIN E.H., *Organizational Culture and Leadership*, 2nd ed., Jossey-Bass, San Francisco, CA, 1992.

[SCH 96] SCHEIN E.H., "Culture: the missing concept in organization studies", *Administrative Sciences Quarterly*, vol. 41, no. 2, pp. 229–240, 1996.

[SCH 04a] SCHEIN E.H., *Organizational Culture and Leadership*, 3rd ed., Jossey-Bass, San Francisco, CA, 2004.

[SCH 04b] SCHEIN E.H., "Organizational Climate and Culture", in *Encyclopedia of Leadership*, Sage Publications, London, 2004.

[SEL 77] SELLTIZ C., WRIGHTSMAN L.S., COOK S.W., *Les méthodes de recherches en sciences sociales*, HRW Editions, Montreal, 1977.

[SEN 90] SENGE P., *The Fifth Discipline: the Art and Practice of the Learning Organisation*, Doubleday, New York, 1990.

[SEN 91] SENGE P., *La cinquième discipline – L'art et la manière des organisations qui apprennent*, Editions First, Paris, 1991.

[SEN 00] SENGE P., ROBERTS C., ROSS R. *et al.*, *Cinquième discipline: le guide du terrain: stratégies et outils pour construire une organisation apprenante*, Editions First, Paris, 2000.

[SHA 97] SHARP J., Key hypotheses in supporting communities of practice, available at: http://www.tfriend.com/hypothesis.html, 1997.

[SIL 00] SILVERMAN D., "Analyzing talk and text", in DENZIN N.K., LINCOLN Y.S. (eds), *Handbook of Qualitative Research*, Sage Publications, Thousand Oaks, CA, 2000.

[SIM 91] SIMON H.A., "Bounded rationality and organizational learning", *Organization Science*, vol. 2, no. 1, pp. 125–134, 1991.

[SKI 74] SKINNER B.F., *About Behaviorism*, Alfred A. Knopf, New York, 1974.

[STA 89] STAR S.L., "The structure of ill-structured solutions: Boundary objects and heterogeneous distributed problem solving", in GASSER L., HUHNS M.N. (eds), *Distributed Artificial Intelligence*, Pitman, London, England, 37–54, 1989.

[STA 96] STATA R., "Organizational learning – the key to mangement innovation", in STARKEY K. (ed.), *How Organizations Learn*, International Thompson Business Press, London, 1996.

[STE 95] STEIN E., "Organizational memory: review of concepts and recommendations for management", *International Journal of Information Management*, vol. 15, no. 2, pp. 17–32, 1995.

[STE 00] STEWART G.L., BARRICK M.R., "Team structure and performance: assessing the mediating role of intrateam process and the moderating role of task type", *Academy of Management Journal*, vol. 43, no. 2, pp. 135–148, 2000.

[STO 92] STOHR E.A., KONSYNSKI B.R., *Information Systems and Decision Processes*, IEEE Computer Society Press, Los Alamitos, CA, 1992.

[STR 97] STRAUB D., KEIL M., BRENNER W., "Testing the technology acceptance model across culture: a three country study", *Information & Management*, vol. 33, no. 1, pp. 1–11, 1997.

[SZU 04] SZULANSKI G., CAPPETTA R., JENSEN, R; J., "When and how trustworthiness matters: knowledge transfer and the moderating effect of causal ambiguity", *Organization Science*, vol. 15, no. 5, pp. 600–613, 2004.

[TAY 95] TAYLOR S., TODD P.A., "Understanding information technology usage: a test of competing models", *Information Systems Research*, vol. 6, no. 2, June, pp. 144–176, 1995.

[TEE 94] TEECE D.J., PISANO G., "The dynamic capabilities of firms: an introduction", *Industrial and Corporate Change*, vol. 3, no. 3, pp. 537–556, 1994.

[TEE 97] TEECE D.J., PISANO G., SHUEN A., "Dynamic capabilities and strategic management", *Strategic Management Journal*, vol. 18, no. 7, pp. 509–534, 1997.

[DET 99] DE TERSSAC G., *Savoirs, compétences, et travail*, Octares, Toulouse, 1999.

[THE 86] THEVENET M., *Audit de la culture d'entreprise*, Editions d'Organisation, Paris, 1989.

[THI 03] THIETARD R.A., *Méthodes de recherche en Management*, Editions Dunod, Paris, 2003.

[THI 96] THIETART R.A. *et al.*, *Méthodes de recherche en Management*, Editions Dunod, Paris, 1996.

[THO 67] THOMPSON J., *Organizations in Action*, McGraw-Hill, New York, 1967.

[THO 91] THOMPSON R.L., HIGGINS C.H., HOWELL J.M., "Towards a conceptual model of utilization", *MIS Quarterly*, vol. 15, no. 1, March, pp. 125–143, 1991.

[TJO 84] TJOSVOLD D., "Cooperation, theory and organizations", *Human Relations*, vol. 37, no. 9, pp. 743–767, 1984.

[TRE 05] TREMBLAY D-G., "Les communautés de pratiques: une analyse différenciée selon le sexe de ce mode d'apprentissage", *Education et francophonie*, vol. 13, no. 1, 2005.

[TRI 80] TRIANDIS H.C., "Values, attitudes, and interpersonal behavior," in HOWE H.E., *Nebraska Symposium on Motivation, 1979*: *Beliefs, Attitudes and Values*, University of Nebraska Press, Lincoln, 1980.

[TRO 98] TROMPENAARS F., *Riding the Waves of Culture: Understanding Diversity in Global Business*, 2nd ed., McGraw-Hill, New York, 1998.

[VAA 02] VAAST E., "Les communautés de pratique sont-elles pertinentes?", *Actes de la 11ème conférence de l'Association Internationale de Management Stratégique*, Paris, 2002.

[VAA 00] VAAST E., "Intranet et aléas organisationnels", *Réseaux*, vol. 18, no. 104, pp. 159–184, 2000.

[VAN 05] VAN BAALEN P., BLOEMHOF-RUWAARD J., VAN HECK E., "Knowledge sharing in an emerging network of practice: the role of a knowledge portal", *European Management Journal*, vol. 23, no. 3, pp. 300–314, 2005.

[VAN 90] VAN DE VEN A., HUBER G.P., "Longitudinal field research methods for studying processes of organizational change", *Organization Science*, vol. 1, no. 3, pp. 213–219, 1990.

[VAN 97] VANCE D., "Information, knowledge and wisdom: the epistic hierarchy and computer-based information systems", *Proceedings of the AIS'97 Conference*, 1997.

[VAN 14] VAN GENDEREN E., "Strategic Knowledge Sharing: Culture Acting as an Inhibitor", *Middle East Journal of Business*, vol. 9, no. 4, pp. 3–8, 2014.

[VEN 99] VENKATESH V., SMITH R.H., "Creation of favourable user perceptions: exploring the role of intrinsic motivation", *MIS Quarterly*, vol. 23, no. 2, pp. 239–260, 1999.

[VOG 01] VOGEL D.R., VAN GENUCHTEN M., LOU D. *et al.*, "Exploratory resarch on the role of national and professional cultures in distributed learning project", *IEEE Transactions on Professional Communication*, vol. 44, no. 2, pp. 114–125, 2001.

[WAC 96] WACHEUX F., *Méthodes Qualitatives et recherches en Gestion*, Editions Economica, Paris, 1996.

[WAG 95] WAGEMAN R., "Interdependence and group effectiveness", *Administrative Science Quarterly*, vol. 40, no. 1, pp. 145–180, 1995.

[WAL 91] WALSH J.P., UNGSON G.R., "Organizational memory", *Academy of Management Review*, vol. 16, no. 1, pp. 57–91, 1991.

[WAT 06] WATSON S., HEWETT K., "A multi theoretical model of knowledge transfer in organizations: determinants of knowledge contribution and knowledge reuse", *Journal of Management Studies*, vol. 43, no. 2, pp. 141–173, 2006.

[WEI 79] WEICK K.E., *The Social Psychology of Organizing*, Addison-Wesley, Reading, MA, 1979.

[WEI 03] WEICK K.E., SUTCLIFFE K.M., "Hospitals as cultures of entrapment: a re-analysis of the Bristol Royal Infirmary", *California Management Review*, vol. 45, no. 2, pp. 73–84, 2003.

[WEN 13] WENDLING M., "Knowledge sharing barriers in global teams", *Journal of Systems and Information Technology*, vol. 15, no. 3, pp. 239–253, 2013.

[WEN 98a] WENGER E., "Communities of practice learning as a social system", *Systems Thinker*, vol. 9, no. 5, pp. 1–5, 1998.

[WEN 98b] WENGER E., *Communities of Practice, Learning, Meaning and Identity*, Cambridge University Press, Cambridge, 1998.

[WEN 02] WENGER E., "Knowledge Management Takes Community Spirit", *CIO*, 2002.

[WEN 00] WENGER E., SNYDER W.M., "Communities of practices: the organizational frontier", *Harvard Business Review*, pp. 139–145, 2000.

[WEN 03] WENGER E., HUYSMAN M., WULF V., "Communities and technologies", *Proceedings of the First International Conference on Communities and Technologies*, 2003.

[WEN 02] WENGER E., MCDERMOTT R., SNYDER W.M., *Cultivating Communities of Practice*, Harvard Business School Press, Boston, MA, 2002.

[WIE 13] WIEWIORA A., TRIGUNARSYAH B., MURPHY G., *et al.*, "Organizational culture and willingness to share knowledge: a competing values perspective in Australian context", *International Journal of Project Management*, vol. 38, no. 8, pp. 1163–1174, 2013.

[WTO 01] WTO, Rapport annuel 2001, Publications de l'OMC, Geneva, 2001.

[WTO 08] WTO, Rapport sur le commerce mondial 2008: Le commerce à l'heure de la mondialisation, Publications de l'OMC, Geneva, 2008.

[YIN 84] YIN R.K., *Case Study Research, Design and Methods*, Sage Publications, Newbury Park, CA, 1984.

[YIN 89] YIN R.K., *Case Study Research, Design and Methods*, Sage, Newbury Park, CA, 1989.

[YIN 03a] YIN R.K., *Applications of Case Study Research*, 2nd ed., Sage Publications, Thousand Oaks, CA, 2003.

[YIN 03b] YIN R.K., *Case Study Research, Design and Methods*, 3rd ed., Sage Publications, Thousand Oaks, CA, 2003.

[YOO 07] YOO Y., LYYTINEN K., HEO D., "Closing the gap: towards a process model of post-merger knowledge sharing", *Information Systems Journal*, vol. 17, no. 4, pp. 321–347, 2007.

[YUS 04] YU S-H., KIM Y-G., KIM M-Y., "Linking organizational knowledge management drivers to knowledge management performance: an exploratory study", *Proceedings of the 37th Hawaii International Conference on System Sciences*, IEEE Computer Society, 2004.

[ZAC 99] ZACK M.H., "Managing codified knowledge", *Sloan Management Review*, vol. 40, no. 4, pp. 45–58, 1999.

[ZAH 98] ZAHEER A., MCEVILY B., PERRONE V., "Does trust matter? Exploring the effects of interorganizational and interpersonal trust on performance", *Organization Science*, vol. 9, no. 2, pp. 141–159, 1998.

[ZAN 95] ZANDER U., KOGUT B., "Knowledge and the speed of the transfer and imitation of organizational capabilities, and empirical test", *Organization Science*, vol. 6, no. 1, pp. 76–92, 1995.

Index

Other titles from

in

Information Systems, Web and Pervasive Computing

2015

ARDUIN Pierre-Emmanuel, GRUNDSTEIN Michel,
ROSENTHAL-SABROUX Camille
Information and Knowledge System
(Advances in Information Systems Set – Volume 2)

BÉRANGER Jérôme
Medical Information Systems Ethics

BRONNER Gérald
Belief and Misbelief Asymmetry on the Internet

IAFRATE Fernando
From Big Data to Smart Data
(Advances in Information Systems Set – Volume 1)

KITAJIMA Munéo
Memory and Action Selection in Human–Machine Interaction
(Human-Machine Interaction Set – Volume 1)

KRICHEN Saoussen, BEN JOUIDA Sihem
Supply Chain Management and its Applications in Computer Science

LEBRATY Jean-Fabrice, LOBRE-LEBRATY Katia
Crowdsourcing: One Step Beyond

SALLABERRY Christian
Geographical Information Retrieval in Textual Corpora

2012

BUCHER Bénédicte, LE BER Florence
Innovative Software Development in GIS

GAUSSIER Eric, YVON François
Textual Information Access

STOCKINGER Peter
Audiovisual Archives: Digital Text and Discourse Analysis

VENTRE Daniel
Cyber Conflict

2011

BANOS Arnaud, THÉVENIN Thomas
Geographical Information and Urban Transport Systems

DAUPHINÉ André
Fractal Geography

LEMBERGER Pirmin, MOREL Mederic
Managing Complexity of Information Systems

STOCKINGER Peter
Introduction to Audiovisual Archives

STOCKINGER Peter
Digital Audiovisual Archives

VENTRE Daniel
Cyberwar and Information Warfare

2010

BONNET Pierre
Enterprise Data Governance

BRUNET Roger
Sustainable Geography

CARREGA Pierre
Geographical Information and Climatology

CAUVIN Colette, ESCOBAR Francisco, SERRADJ Aziz
Thematic Cartography – 3-volume series
Thematic Cartography and Transformations – volume 1
Cartography and the Impact of the Quantitative Revolution – volume 2
New Approaches in Thematic Cartography – volume 3

LANGLOIS Patrice
Simulation of Complex Systems in GIS

MATHIS Philippe
Graphs and Networks – 2nd edition

THERIAULT Marius, DES ROSIERS François
Modeling Urban Dynamics

2009

BONNET Pierre, DETAVERNIER Jean-Michel, VAUQUIER Dominique
Sustainable IT Architecture: the Progressive Way of Overhauling Information Systems with SOA

PAPY Fabrice
Information Science

RIVARD François, ABOU HARB Georges, MERET Philippe
The Transverse Information System

ROCHE Stéphane, CARON Claude
Organizational Facets of GIS

VENTRE Daniel
Information Warfare

2008

BRUGNOT Gérard
Spatial Management of Risks

FINKE Gerd
Operations Research and Networks

GUERMOND Yves
Modeling Process in Geography

KANEVSKI Michael
Advanced Mapping of Environmental Data

MANOUVRIER Bernard, LAURENT Ménard
Application Integration: EAI, B2B, BPM and SOA

PAPY Fabrice
Digital Libraries

2007

DOBESCH Hartwig, DUMOLARD Pierre, DYRAS Izabela
Spatial Interpolation for Climate Data

SANDERS Lena
Models in Spatial Analysis

2006

CLIQUET Gérard
Geomarketing

CORNIOU Jean-Pierre
Looking Back and Going Forward in IT

DEVILLERS Rodolphe, JEANSOULIN Robert
Fundamentals of Spatial Data Quality

Lightning Source UK Ltd.
Milton Keynes UK
UKHW02n2034091018
330257UK00003B/127/P